CAREERS IN
MUSIC

Also by Gene Busnar

SUPER STARS OF ROCK
Their Lives and Their Music

IT'S ROCK 'N' ROLL
A Musical History of the Fabulous Fifties

CAREERS IN
MUSIC
Gene Busnar

SALEM LUTHERAN CHURCH & SCHOOL
SOUTHEAST AT BEECHER AVE.
JACKSONVILLE, ILLINOIS 62650

JULIAN MESSNER
NEW YORK

Copyright © 1982 by Eugene Busnar
All rights reserved including the right of
reproduction in whole or in part in any form.
Published by Julian Messner, a Simon & Schuster
Division of Gulf & Western Corporation,
Simon & Schuster Building,
1230 Avenue of the Americas,
New York, New York 10020.
JULIAN MESSNER and colophon are trademarks of
Simon & Schuster, registered in the U.S. Patent
and Trademark Office.

Manufactured in the United States of America.
Design by Irving Perkins Associates

Library of Congress Cataloging in Publication Data

Busnar, Gene.
Careers in music.

Bibliography: p. 249
Includes index.
1. Music—Economic aspects.   2. Music
trade—United States.   I. Title.
ML3795.B95   780'.23'73   82-2290
ISBN 0-671-42410-6   AACR2

Contents

To the memory of the late David Izenson

Acknowledgments

I would like to thank Matt Biberfeld of radio station WNCN in New York for allowing me to use the following taped interviews from his "Metropolitan Arts" program: Simon Estes, Harold Shaw, Elliott Galkin and Victoria Bond. Special thanks to Alan Grubman who opened so many doors for me in the popular music field and Audrey Michaels who did the same service in the area of classical music.

Much of the information in this book came from first-hand interviews. The following people gave generously of their time and insights. I owe them each a debt of gratitude for their unique contributions to the shaping of this book: Adele Scheele, Junior Walker, Phillip Namanworth, Genya Ravan, Roger Probert, Mark Schimmel, Charles Koppelman, Sandy Linzer, Doug Frank, Jeanne Napoli, Tom Mattola, Niles Siegel, Doug Pell, Seymour Feig, Sid Bernstein, Ray Reneri, Gerard Schwarz, Peter Mennin, Michael Wilcok, Victoria Bond, Sung Rai Sohn, Morton Gould, Sheldon Gold, Lois Schweitzer, Patricia Sohn, Gabriel Kosakoff, Allan Atlas, Shirley Flemming, Roman Kozack, Herb Karlitz, Sylvia Kraft, Jim Cameron, Mark Chernoff, Pete Fornatel, Bob Mahlman, Walter Sabo, Bob Vanderheyden, Brad Leigh, Roger Sadowsky, and Christopher Jaffe. (The comments of Rise Stevens, Richard Graham, William Anderson, and Thomas Willis originally

7

appeared in the *Careers and Music* edition of the "Music Educators Journal").

Special thanks to John Sposato, Kitty Lance, John Kois, Paul Wilson, Allison Blackman, Seth Flagsberg, Jamie Forbes, Henry Kavett, and Mrs. Wasser of the U.S. Department of Labor. Finally, I would like to express my appreciation for the tremendous help and patience of my loving wife Elizabeth.

Introduction

On the surface, music is one of those glamour professions that inspires the fantasies of the public. Top performers make lots of money and are among our greatest heroes. There are literally thousands of young people planning to be the next Paul McCartney, Linda Ronstadt, or Zubin Mehta. Few will ever achieve this kind of superstar status. And even those who do rise to the top will first have to pay their dues. Do you want to be a rock 'n' roll star? Then be prepared to struggle for many years before you are even in a position to get noticed. Do you long to be the conductor of one of the world's great symphony orchestras? Get ready to put in years of practice and accept the possibility that you will wind up just one of thousands of talented people who is not quite good enough to work at the highest levels.

Many successful people involved with music also once dreamed of becoming performers. Some of them did. Others became recording engineers, music critics, artist managers, and high school music teachers. They are not the people in the limelight. But they have the satisfaction of playing a part in the making of music that is every bit as important as the contribution of a performer. The greatest group in the world will get nowhere in today's music business without the help of a skilled manager. The most talented opera singer can not develop his or her voice properly without the aid of an equally talented singing teacher. Furthermore, no performers in any musical style will become recognized unless they are signed by a record company and get their music played by radio stations. The people you will meet in this book are professionals in music and music-related careers. They work in technical fields like instrument building and business fields like orchestra administration. Some of them earn close to a million dollars a year and others struggle to pay their rent. Together, their personal stories and insights cover a wide range of possibilities in the fields of popular music, classical music, the music business, music education, radio, music writing, and technical careers. Each career section begins with a fact sheet which summarizes the basic facts of the various occupations. Information for the fact sheets was compiled from government and private agencies, unions and guilds, and the firsthand knowledge of professionals in the various fields. The sections conclude with a listing of organizations and publications that provide further information.

No book on careers would be complete without a general discussion of the issues involved in making a successful career. Part I of the book explores these issues in some detail. Although the discussion is geared toward careers in music, the skills for making a successful career are much the same in any area. The materials in this section provide a framework for the reader to evaluate his or her own plan of action in a logical and realistic way.

Who should read this book? Certainly, anyone interested in some phase of the music business as a career. But these pages should also interest anybody who has a general interest in the workings of a rock band, a classical orchestra, or a radio station. Because many careers in music are competitive and relatively closed, the techniques that people use to break in and get ahead are a good starting point for anyone planning to build a successful career in any field.

CAREERS IN
MUSIC

CHAPTER 1

Speaking of Careers

CAREER FACTS

Before we explore the major career areas in music and music-related fields, let's pinpoint the things people need to know when they attempt to pursue any career. There are three basic areas we need to explore; three general questions that cover a wide range of issues.

1) *What are the facts about the career/careers that I have in mind?*
2) *Do I have what it takes to be a success in a given career?*
3) *What skills does a person need to be a success at any career?*

The facts about any career consist of pieces of information that round out the picture of what it is like to work in a particular field. These include:

Definition and Description

What the job actually entails. What the duties and responsibilities are of a person doing that kind of work.

Education and Training

There are tremendous differences in the type and amount of formal education that people need to be successful in music and music-related areas. Most classical performers attend a conservatory or university. Some careers in education and administration require advanced degrees. Many of our best rock musicians have little or no formal musical training. They learned their craft by working in small clubs and hanging around better and more experienced musicians. Always remember that there are many ways to get "schooled" outside of the classroom. Many successful people in radio broadcasting and recording engineering took part-time jobs when they were teenagers—going for coffee and sweeping up. Some went to college. But there are also a number of highly respected people in these careers who never went beyond high school.

The information in this book will serve as a basic guide to the best ways of selecting a music teacher, researching a college or training program, and deciding how much formal education to pursue. But each person must find his or her own road. There are very few easy answers or straight and narrow paths. Each person will have to do his or her own research and come to individual conclusions.

Chances of Success

No matter how competitive or closed a field might seem, there is always a need for talented young people. Still, you had better know what the opportunities are and what the future outlook is. Performing fields are always the toughest because so many people are always trying to get into these so-called glamour areas. Even in more open fields like music therapy and classical music management, people rarely just waltz into a position. There is tremendous competition for almost every decent job in today's tight market. If you are going to have to put in a great deal of effort anyway, you might as well explore those career areas that really interest you. Most successful people are not easily discouraged. They are ready to work hard to achieve their goals. As we will see, it is not only how hard they work but also the way they work that makes them successful.

Financial

Compared to other factors, how important is money to you? Most people who go into a field like music education do not plan to get rich. But aspiring rock performers often dream of untold riches. To get a true picture, you can not just look at the incomes of a Paul McCartney or a Linda Ronstadt. You have also got to consider the many talented people who must support themselves by driving taxis and waitering.

Lifestyle

Are you a "night person?" If the answer is no, don't plan to be a rock musician. Do you like to travel? Most performers—including the most successful ones—spend a great deal of time on the road. People in the classical field constantly point to talented musicians who gave up their positions with major orchestras because they could not take the rigors of traveling. Can you work on your own for months at a time? People who perform or compose must have the self-discipline to practice or write their music with no supervision. Are you capable of working around the clock? Recording engineers must often go for days at a time with little or no sleep. They often have to work on holidays and weekends and have little time for a "normal" family life. Before you select any career, you must be aware of the demands of that lifestyle.

Working Conditions

Before you enter a field, you should know where you are likely to be working, who your co-workers will be, what the hours are, and what additional responsibilities you might have to assume. Most well-known rock performers started out working in small clubs for low pay, rehearsing in garages, and leading lives of uncertainty. Music therapists have to work in hospital settings helping people with emotional problems. Successful music-business lawyers are bombarded with phone calls from morning until night. Managers have to be prepared to be woken out of a deep sleep by a performer whose car has broken down on the road. Jazz musicians have to tolerate audiences that are more interested in ordering drinks and talking than in listening to the music. Major conductors in the classical field must answer to a board of directors if a concert hall does not sell out or if the musical selections are not well-received by important critics. Most of the best-known radio disc jockeys have no say over the music they play. They are usually handed a play-list by the station's program director and have no freedom of choice.

Most of the facts about any career lie below the surface. You might be surprised to discover the kinds of problems involved in the various careers. But you had better know what these facts are if you intend to make intelligent career choices.

Once you learn about what is involved in a particular career, you must ask yourself if you have what it takes to be happy and successful in that kind of work. Finding yourself is far more difficult than learning the facts about a career. People often have to go through a number of careers before they settle into the one that is right for them. But it is important that you learn to evaluate your abilities and feelings as soon as you can. Here are some things you ought to consider in deciding if a particular career is right for you.

Talent

Success in any career requires some kind of talent. Many people compensate for a lack of natural ability by trying harder. But if you are going to get ahead in a difficult and competitive area like classical performing or composing, you must have a tremendous amount of natural talent *and* work extremely hard to perfect your skills. In other fields, talent might play a smaller part in the formula for success, but it is always a factor.

If you want to find out how much talent you have in a given area, try to get involved as soon as possible. If you feel you can be a performer, find a good teacher and practice as hard as you can. If you think you have what it takes to be a disc jockey, make tapes of yourself at home and start developing your skills. If management appeals to you, offer your services to a local talent agency. In other words, develop your talent by exercising your skills. Even if you eventually find that you do not have enough talent to be a successful professional, you will have developed skills that might help you in another area. This is especially true in music-related fields where aspiring performers often become successful managers, critics, or teachers.

Desire

No matter how much talent you might have, you are not likely to get anywhere unless you are willing to devote a great deal of time and energy to developing that talent.

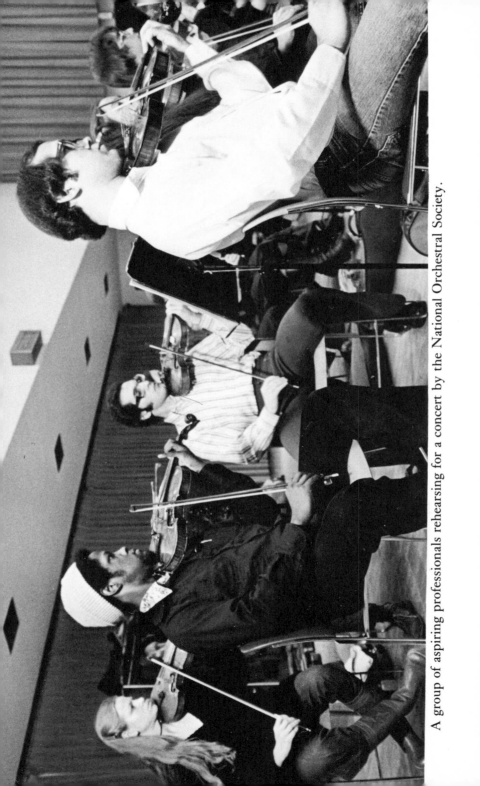

A group of aspiring professionals rehearsing for a concert by the National Orchestral Society.

Many of the professionals interviewed for this book advise people not to even consider competitive fields like performing and composing unless they have it "in their blood." Even in more open fields like management and broadcasting, the advice is pretty much the same. "Don't even think about it unless you are truly driven to be in the field."

Most of the rewarding careers in music are not nine-to-five type jobs. You can hardly separate your work life from your personal life. If you are a musician, you have to rehearse. So you tend to spend more time with your co-workers than people on most jobs. You also have to spend a good deal of time practicing your instrument. This type of involvement is also true of people in many other music-related areas.

If you are an aspiring performer, you must ask yourself some hard questions at an early stage: Are you willing to devote thousands of hours to practicing, knowing that you may never be able to become a professional classical musician? Although the practice time is usually far less for successful rock musicians, years of rejection and frustration are the rule before one can receive the rewards of success. Are you dedicated enough to stick it out in spite of your friends and family telling you that you are wasting your time?

Physical and Emotional Strength

Let's say you have the talent and the dedication to be a successful performer. Are you strong enough to withstand the rigors of what insiders call "the life." Let's look at a typical forty-eight hours in the life of a well-known rhythm and blues musician.

Junior Walker is a highly respected singer/saxophone player who has spent the better part of the last twenty years making records and touring. Although his records no

Singer/saxophonist Junior Walker poses for a publicity shot. (NEAL HOLLANDR COLLECTION)

longer grace the hit parade, he had a string of hits for the Motown label during the 60's and 70's. Now well into his forties, Junior Walker still performs with a vital energy that has maintained his popularity as a club performer. Here is a recent two-day travelog:

Thursday night—Play two one-hour sets in Detroit
Friday morning—Get up at 6 A.M. and drive 700 miles to New York
Friday night—Play one ninety-minute set
Saturday morning—Wake up, give an interview, pack up
Saturday afternoon—Drive 200 miles to Boston
Saturday night—Play two one-hour sets

Junior Walker claims that he loves this kind of life. He wouldn't want it any other way. But do you think most people in their forties would have the physical strength to be happy with this lifestyle?

Aside from being strong of body, performers also must withstand a great deal of emotional pressure. Henry Fogel, orchestra manager of the New York Philharmonic, recalls that a doctor found the blood pressure of orchestra members before and after a rehearsal was much higher than normal. Imagine how much more tension is involved in an actual performance? Let's look at the story of a talented and dedicated young musician who did not have the emotional strength to pursue the life of a performer.

The career of a solo performer in the classical field is among the most difficult and demanding of all the careers in music. No matter how much native talent a person may have, there is no getting around the years of formal study and solitary practicing that are necessary to begin seriously thinking of becoming a classical soloist. A successful person in this field needs a tremendous amount of inborn talent and the discipline and desire to practice at least five hours a day. And this is just the beginning. The few soloists who actually make this work their primary career must also have a tremendous amount of luck, as well as tens of thousands of dollars for lessons, first-rate instruments, accompanying musicians, wardrobes, etc.

On the surface, it would seem that Joel had all of the ingredients. From the time he was ten, it was apparent to his parents and teachers that he had an extraordinary talent for classical music. After entering New York's High School of Music and Art, Joel also developed an interest in jazz piano and displayed a remarkable ability for improvisation. But Joel's greatest strength was as a classical concertina player. Partly because of the relatively small number of competitors on this neglected instrument, Joel was considered to be one of the top ten concertina players in America by the time he entered college. But the young man felt rather uneasy about performing. After receiving his degree from a good liberal arts college, Joel decided to pursue a doctorate in musicology (the systematic study of the science, history, forms, and methods of music).

Normally, Joel's parents would have been delighted with their son's decision to enter the academic world. But these were wealthy people who took an active part in New York's exciting cultural scene. Because they genuinely appreciated his rare talent, Joel's folks wanted to do all they could to help their son reach the stage of Carnegie Hall. They felt that their high financial standing would remove any of the pressures that aspiring performers usually have to endure. But Joel was burdened with other pressures—those which come from undue emotional strain.

In accordance with his parents' wishes, Joel took a year off from his studies in order to perform a series of solo concerts on the East coast. His performances were well-received by critics, but Joel often seemed totally drained after a performance. In everyday life, Joel was a friendly, easygoing person who enjoyed going to a ball game or a good restaurant. But when he took the stage, he seemed to enter an ecstatic dream world. As he played the works of Beethoven, Bach, and Haydn, he would close his eyes and move his head and body in a trance-like manner. After the concerts, he would be physically and emotionally drained. As he began working the better concert halls, the tension became worse. On two occasions, Joel fainted immediately after leaving the stage.

Because of the excellent reviews and his parents' influence, Joel received a booking at Carnegie Hall. Friends and family members were all concerned about Joel's fainting spells. But Joel had no intention of backing out of this opportunity, which so few musicians ever get: A solo performance at Carnegie Hall.

When the big night finally arrived, Joel seemed in a rather good mood. The program was going well, although Joel had been in greater command of his music on other occasions. Suddenly, during the next-to-last number in the concert, Joel collapsed on the Carnegie Hall stage. He was revived in just a few minutes. But a potentially great concert career had come to an abrupt end.

It is ironic that several major newspapers gave Joel a much bigger write-up than they would have if he had not fainted. His services were in greater demand than ever. But Joel had made a final decision. He did not have the emotional strength to be a performer. He would finish his studies in musicology and pursue a life in the academic side of music.

Today, Joel is a teacher at one of the better liberal arts universities on the West coast. He has no regrets about the past. "If I wouldn't have tried to be a performer, I would always have been frustrated," he says now. "I still love music and I'm glad I had so many rare opportunities. But I think the key for any young person is to evaluate his skills and emotions early in the game. This goes double for anyone considering a career as a performer."

SECRETS OF SUCCESS

In any career, there are only a small number of men and women at the top. These people are always questioned about their success. There is often a suspicion that some of those at the top were lucky or even ruthless in their rise. There are, in fact, people in every field who were placed in a high position by a relative. But truly successful people must do many things on their own to rise to the top. Unfortunately, these people usually can not say just what it is they do that makes them so successful. Their skills are not things that are generally taught in school. So how does a young person go about learning these so-called secrets of success?

Dr. Adele Scheele is a well-known career coach who has pinpointed a number of things that successful people have in common. In her book, *Skills For Success*, Dr. Scheele focuses on three general skills that young people need to develop to achieve their career goals. These are self-presentation, positioning, and connecting.

Self-Presentation

How one presents oneself to others is a key factor in every aspect of life. This begins with obvious things like making a good appearance and knowing how to talk with people. Even in a highly skilled career like classical performing, there is a lot more than musical talent involved. Nobody would deny that all of the great conductors or classical soloists are people of enormous musical accomplishment. But those who become "stars" have a lot more going for them. Here is what Harold Shaw, one of the most important managers in the classical field, has to say about presenting oneself correctly:

A soloist must have the ability to perform in addition to musical ability. There's a great deal of difference between a player and a performer. Many artists play very well but they don't give a performance. And if you're going to have a public performance career, you must have public performance qualities. . . . There must be some kind of a spark that captures the audience.

That *spark* must come across for people to be successful in any area. Consider that the ability of a classical musician is easier to judge than the talents of people in most other areas. But Dr. Scheele points out that all successful people have good self-presentation qualities.

When you go to present yourself, you only have a very short time to make the right impression. . . . If you ask successful people what they did that day, they will say they had meetings, talked on the phone or whatever. But that doesn't begin to tell you what they do in those meetings and phone calls that pulls it all together for them. . . . If you could listen in on the conversations that a top conductor has with his orchestra or a powerful manager has with a record company, you would pick up on the strong self-presentation skills that help make these people successful.

Executives like Jim Cameron of NBC Source Radio can size up a person's potential in a few short minutes.

When I'm interviewing someone, I can tell if that person is going to do well here within five minutes. . . . You've got to be hungry and you've got to be interested in learning as much as you can. I can recognize a kind of curiosity that makes a person curious about every aspect of this business. So I know the kind of person that will sit down and try to fix a tape machine if it breaks down. . . . That same kind of person will sit down after hours with the chief engineer and learn how to mix records. And he won't be too proud to go out and get a cup of coffee if that's what he's asked to do.

SALEM LUTHERAN CHURCH & SCHOOL
SOUTHEAST AT BEECHER AVE.
JACKSONVILLE, ILLINOIS   62650

How does one develop the skills involved in good self-presentation? There are specific abilities like talking on the phone and writing letters which can be developed through practice. But the qualities that Jim Cameron speaks of—things like enthusiasm, versatility, and sensitivity—come from dealing with people in a variety of real life situations. Some of these experiences can be found in school—both in classes and in extracurricular activities. But in many cases, young people must go outside of the school setting.

Dr. Scheele believes that young people ought to get involved in as many activities as possible in order to develop the skills and the personal courage that are so important throughout one's life. She also feels that there are always opportunities for young people to get involved in areas they have an interest in. And if opportunities do not present themselves to you, it is your responsibility to go out and make them.

"Get involved in school activities," Dr. Scheele urges. "Try to get a job in something you're interested in after school. If you want to write about music, write a column in the school newspaper. Or offer to do a free review for a small local paper. If there isn't a newspaper, start your own music pamphlet. Or go to the local music store and write a pamphlet for them. These things take energy and they take courage. *But the only way you're going to learn to do is by doing.*"

Positioning

Almost every successful person mentions good timing as an important element of success. There is no doubt that luck is important, and timing is a big part of being lucky. There are lots of familiar sayings like: *Be at the right place at the right time* and *I'd rather be lucky than good* that stress the importance of good timing.

People often believe that they have no control over their

luck. They look at those at the top of their fields and say, "There but for the grace of God go I." But a careful look at successful people shows that there are many things that can be done to help your luck along. The story of Roger Probert, an executive at Atlantic Records artist development division, shows the kinds of things that successful people do when they find themselves in the right place at the right time. Roger recalls:

I was a bass player in a fairly successful English rock band. But we never got over the hump of having a hit record. So after a while we broke up. I was broke and needed some kind of temporary work—anything! As it happened, they needed some temporary help at Atlantic Records. I guess they liked me because they offered me a full-time job.

Here I was, twenty-seven years old, an ex-musician with no other skills. But I took this job as a goffer. I told my boss that I planned to do the job better than anyone else had ever done it. He said, "If you really do a great job people will notice and you'll get ahead." Here I am a few years later with a really interesting job finding new talent for the label.

For the most part, people who find themselves in the right place at the right time also had experiences being at the right place at the wrong time, at the wrong place at the right time, and at the wrong place at the wrong time. They learned how to get ahead from being in different situations. It's not only that they hang in and try again. Somehow, successful people learn how to try again in different ways. Again, there is no exact formula for success other than pursuing a number of experiences and learning from them.

Connecting

Have you ever heard the phrase, "It's not what you know but who you know"? There is no doubt that people often get jobs through their families and friends. Those of us who are not so lucky might feel that this is unfair. But as

Dr. Scheele points out, "Life isn't fair. Somehow we all grow up learning that things are supposed to be fair. But if you look around, you see that's just not the way things work."

Let's face it. You are going to need contacts to get ahead in this world. This does not mean that you have to be born into a rich, influential family. Like anything else, making contacts is a skill you can develop. You would do well to begin making your contacts as soon as possible. Here are some tips from Dr. Scheele on how to begin making connections in a field you are interested in.

> If you want to emulate a particular musician, offer to carry his bags or clean his equipment. Try to be around so you can learn as much as possible. If you approach a few people and they reject you, think about changing your approach. Maybe you are approaching people who are too busy. If so, just try someone who is less busy.

> Most people will stop for interviews. Try to interview someone for the school paper whose career interests you. If you're not on the paper, you can try to get an assembly together and be on the programming committee. Try to get some musicians and people on the administrative end to be part of a panel. Pick the person on that panel who interests you and stick with that person. Call that person or write a letter and ask if you can come over and talk to him or help him in some way.

> The people you approach are liable to be very busy. So you are the one who is going to have to insist on a friendship because they often don't have the time. But you should pursue it, because many people will respond to a young person who is intelligent and up and coming. . . . But nobody will take an interest in a young person who is passive or complains.

Dr. Scheele points out that people sometimes do not pursue contacts because they are shy or are afraid of using people. But connecting with others involves using people in the best sense of the phrase. The same person who helps you with your career today might look upon *you* as a valued contact ten years from now.

Bob Vanderheyden, program director of WCBS-FM in New York, recalls how one of his earliest contacts in radio eventually wound up working for him:

> I developed an interest in theatre and radio when I was in high school. While I was working at the local theatre after school, I met Jack Sterling—a well-known New York disc jockey. After high school, I went into the Marines. When I got out, I had a job lined up at the local radio station in my home town in Connecticut. . . . Two weeks before I got out of the Marines, I ran into Jack Sterling in a local bar. Jack said, "How would you like to come to work at CBS in New York?" I got discharged from the Marines on a Friday. The next Monday I was working in the newsroom at CBS. Later on, I started writing some gag material for Jack and then I became his producer. When Jack left to work at WHN, he asked me to come over there and be his producer. I eventually got to be program manager and program director at that station.

You can practice your connecting skills by speaking to people in a variety of situations. Sometimes a person you meet by chance can turn out to be a valuable contact. Once you establish a contact, keep in touch with that person. Let him know how you are progressing by writing or calling from time to time. If one of your contacts helps you connect to other people, do something to show your appreciation. Keep a file of all your contacts so that you can refer back to them months or even years later. Above all, do not be afraid to reach out to those people who are in a position to help you. Remember, they probably needed the help of others to get where they are.

Now that we have established some general ground rules for pursuing a career, let's take a look at certain problems and issues that come up over and over again in discussing careers in music.

Combining Careers

People in music and music-related fields often pursue several careers. Part of this has to do with branching out within your field. For example, a successful rock musician might want to get involved with the production and management of other creative people. Most of our better classical musicians and conductors spend some time teaching and working with young people.

On the other side of the coin are the many talented people who are unable to make a sufficient living through performing. These people often teach, or they may become involved as agents or technicians. Some well-known musicians decide that it is better to make one's living doing something else and pursue music after working hours. Charles Ives, the highly regarded contemporary composer, became wealthy working in the insurance business. This allowed him to compose without thoughts of how he was going to sell his work. Of course, many of us would not have the energy to devote hours to a demanding activity like composing after putting in a full day's work. But if you are thinking of becoming a performer, you might be wise to have something in mind that you can do to support yourself in case your plans do not work out.

When to Stop Trying

The story of how the Beatles were turned down by almost every record company before they finally got a contract is well-known. We hear it over and over again in the music business. This kind of story gives thousands of aspiring performers hope. Perhaps the next person who hears your tape will decide that your group is the next Beatles. People who are trying to make it as pop stars understand that the odds are stacked against them. But nobody can succeed unless he or she dares to dream.

Dr. Scheele classifies people trying to make it in music into three categories:

One kind of person says, "I'm going to devote my whole life to music no matter how long it takes." That kind of person isn't going to mind driving a taxi or waitering in order to make ends meet because he is so in love with the process of making music.

A second kind of person says, "I'm going to give myself a certain number of years, and if nothing happens I'll get into another field—like business or engineering—where I can use my music background." A lot of people who can't negotiate for themselves are very good at negotiating for others, and they can do well as agents or managers.

A third kind of person says, "If it doesn't work out after a certain number of years, I'll go into something else completely." These people find it too painful to see others doing the thing that they so much wanted to do. But there are usually a lot of right things for each person to do. If you try to do one thing in a lot of different ways and still don't succeed, you have to stop and try something else.

The attempt of finding something else is really what the process of careering is all about. If you think of life as a test . . . that's a lousy way to live. If you decide that if you make it in music you pass, and if you don't make it in music you fail, you are going to have problems. But if instead, you look at life as an experiment, then you try things out and see if they work. If something works, you say, "Great, let's see what else works." If something doesn't work for you, you still haven't failed. That thing may not have worked out. But you're still not a failure as a person.

So it's important to think of careering as an experimental process. It's something like fishing where you can't say you failed. You can just say that you didn't catch anything. This is the way that successful people tend to look at their lives. They never say, "I failed." They just say, "This didn't work out."

Gerard Schwarz, a highly regarded young conductor and former co-principal trumpet player in the New York Philharmonic, remembers the problems one of his advanced trumpet students had in deciding to pursue a full-time career as a classical musician.

> A young lawyer who was studying with me wanted more than anything else to be a musician. He was progressing quite well. But he was a little discouraged because he still had a lot of work to do to be successful on a professional level. . . . Then he was offered a job in a New York law firm. He called me and asked my advice as to whether he should accept the law position or pursue his musical goals.
>
> I said, "Don't take the law position right now. You're a very bright guy and you'll always be able to work as a lawyer. Right now, if you don't go as far as you can on your instrument, you'll never know if you could have made it. A year from now, I'll be better able to tell you." A year from that day, he got a job playing first trumpet in an orchestra in Brazil.
>
> He spent a few years in that orchestra. But he realized that he was never going to be good enough to play in one of the top orchestras. So he came back to the States and took a position as a lawyer, though he still plays a lot. But at the time that he asked me, I couldn't tell him that he wasn't going to make it. It's very hard to tell somebody that he has gone as far as he's going to go.

Putting It All Together

As we look at the lives of successful people in music and music-related fields, we find that many of them have the following things in common:

- An early interest in music
- Correct evaluation of their strengths and weaknesses
- The courage and foresight to find appropriate training grounds on their own

• Well-developed self-presentation, positioning, and connecting skills

Alan Grubman is one of the top five attorneys in the music business. If we follow the progression of his career, we can see that most of the elements that make people successful have entered into the picture. Alan claims that he never sat down and formulated a master plan for his life. But if you analyze his story, you find that he somehow did most of the right things along the way. He credits his "good instincts" for much of his success. Those instincts helped him pull all the ingredients for success together.

> I remember people asking me at seven what I wanted to be when I grew up. I always said, a lawyer. I was born with the gift of gab. . . . If you're a good talker and you're Jewish, your parents will usually tell you to become a lawyer. When I was about eleven, I became a singer on an amateur television show called "The Children's Hour." Being on that show gave me my first taste of show business. It was the first time that I noticed how well people in the entertainment world live. I came from a middle class background. So this was my first exposure to limousines and fancy restaurants.

By the time he was thirteen, Alan's voice changed and he realized that he was not going to become a professional entertainer. But he still wanted to get involved in show business. He first started thinking about entertainment law when he was in high school. "At that time," he admits, "I don't think I even knew what an entertainment lawyer was. But the two things I had on my mind were law and entertainment."

Alan was only an average student in college; he never tried very hard. But he was always a good talker, and someone who was determined to make a lot of money in the future. His career at Brooklyn Law School was also nothing to shout about. But Alan was developing some important skills and contacts for the future.

> The truth is, I was kind of a joke in law school. Most of the other students took jobs in law firms during the summer of their second year. When I told my friends that I was going to work in the mail room of the William Morris talent agency, they thought I was out of my mind. The next year, I took a job as a page at CBS television. I used to come into school with my page uniform, and I was really something of a laughing stock.
>
> I didn't realize it at the time, but I was actually doing exactly what I should have been doing. I was schooling myself in the field I wanted to work in and getting to know people in that field. After law school, I just walked into one of the bigger entertainment law firms and asked them to give me a shot. Money wasn't important at that time, and I even said, "How much can I pay you to let me work here?" But they started me at $125 a week. I didn't have the credentials that people now put on my desk every day. But somehow, I convinced them that it would be worth their time to hire and train me.

From the beginning of his law career, Alan was an extremely hard worker. He also had a good deal of natural talent in negotiating and dealing with people in the entertainment field. People who knew Alan as a mediocre student sometimes express surprise at his rise to the top of his profession. But Alan appears to have known exactly what he was doing.

> I always had this gut feeling that good grades in school really didn't mean that much. I always managed to get by. But truthfully, I had no interest at all in getting straight A's. What does it mean to be a star in school? It means that you get a piece of paper that says A on it. What does it mean to be a star in the real world? It means that you make hundreds of thousands of dollars which allows you to do whatever you want.

But the respect that people give you when you are really good at what you do is even more important than the money. I didn't have that when I was in school, so I appreciate it even more now.

CHAPTER 2

Popular Music and the Music Business

PERFORMING AND SONGWRITING CAREERS

Musician/Singer

GETTING STARTED NOW

If you can sing or play a musical instrument, you can start making a good part-time income while you are still in high school. Many talented young musicians work local parties and dances after only a few months of taking lessons. Singers who have a good feel for popular styles can sometimes break in without any formal training.

The best way to put together a little band is to practice with some other musicians at your level who like the same kinds of music you do. Some bands work from sheet music. Others prefer copying directly from records. However you work, it is usually best to start off with songs that everybody can play. Once you have learned about twenty songs, offer to play for free at a school dance or a friend's party. It is essential to play in front of people as often as possible. No matter how good you sound at rehearsals, you must get used to performing in real-life situations.

If you start going over well with your audiences, you might soon start getting called regularly to play for local functions. At this point, you can set a price for your services. You might also invest some of your earnings in business cards, records, sheet music, musical equipment, and advertising in local papers. It might also be helpful to put different band members in charge of various phases of the operation. One person can be the musical leader. Another member can be in charge of advertising and publicity. A third member can handle booking the jobs and collecting money. If you have a good sound and organize yourselves as a business, you can build your group's reputation in a relatively short time.

Playing in a high school band is a tremendous experience. You get the chance to earn money doing something you enjoy. You are also developing some important skills that can serve you well throughout your life. If you are thinking of becoming a professional musician, you are learning things about your craft that even the best teacher can not give you. The experience you get from being part of a creative and business team carries over into whatever career you eventually decide on.

Many talented people have no interest in continuing their musical careers after high school or college. Others turn their musical skills into a profitable part-time occupation. There are thousands of people in all walks of life who make good money working only on weekends. These individuals do not have to work very hard in order to improve their musical skills, although they do have to keep up with current trends in the musical style(s) they are playing.

FACT SHEET
PERFORMING CAREERS IN POPULAR MUSIC

Career	Opportunities for Employment	Education and Training	Skills and Personality Traits
MUSICIAN	1• Nightclubs (steady employment) 2• Club dates (parties—single engagements) 3• Shows 4• Rock concerts 5• Recording studios (record sessions, commercials, movie soundtracks) 6• Television 7• Houses of worship 8• Armed forces	• No formal degree required but intensive private study helpful • Ability to read music required for Numbers 3, 5, 6, 7 and 8. Desirable for all other kinds of work • Practical experience	• Technical knowledge of instrument(s) • Versatility • Business and public relations skills • Self-discipline • Commitment • Stage presence • Poise • Physical Stamina
SINGER	1• Nightclubs (steady employment) 2• Club dates (parties–single engagements 3• Shows (chorus) 4• Rock concerts 5• Recording studios: A. Soloist B. Background singer C. Radio commercials D. Featured Films and T.V. E. T.V. commercials	• No formal degree required but intensive private study helpful • Ability to read music required for 3 and 5. Desirable for all other kinds of work	• Same as musician plus good singing voice in style(s) in which you are working

Lifestyle	Earnings	Employment Outlook
• Night and week-end work • Considerable time spent in practice and rehearsal • Long and irregular hours • Performances often require travel • Hard to obtain year-round work	1• $350 per 5-night week—5-hour night 2• Approx. $78 to $96 for 4 hours 3• Approx. $360 per week 4• Highly variable 5• Approx. $50 per hour 6• Approx. $212 for a 1-hour show 7• Approx. $20 an hour 8• Base pay as per various military branches	1• and 2• Competitive but less difficult to obtain than other kinds of employment 3• Hard to find steady work 4• Extremely competitive 5• Highly competitive 6• Virtually closed 7• Some part-time work available, few full-time positions 8• Available to qualified applicants
• Same as musician	• Numbers 1–4 same as musician 5A• Approx. $100 per song or per hour—whichever is greater; plus royalties 5B• Approx. $43 per song or per hour whichever is greater 5C• Approx. $104.50 per commercial plus residuals 5D• Approx. $250–$350 per day 5E• Approx. $200 per commercial plus residuals for soloists	1–4• Same as musician 5• Very competitive, and hard to find steady work

Turning Pro

If you have no interest in becoming a serious professional, you can keep working in local bands and make the best out of whatever opportunities come your way. If, however, you plan to make a career as a musician, you had better start sharpening your skills as soon as possible. Talent and musical knowledge are very important. But you will also need contacts, organization, public relations skills, a certain "sense of the street," determination, and a good measure of luck in order to get ahead.

Musical Skills

No matter what instrument you play, you should learn to read music fluently. There are some successful people— particularly singers, guitarists, and drummers—who make an excellent living without the ability to read music. But these people are the exceptions. Their services are in demand because they have an individual style or feel that is truly unique. They have the ability to learn their parts quickly *by ear*. This means that they can play or sing an appropriate part after hearing a new song only once or twice.

Most successful professionals have good reading skills *and* a highly developed ear. An aspiring musician would be wise to do the following: learn music theory; become a good reader; develop lots of technique on your instrument; and play in as many different situations as you can. The more things you can do well, the more your services will be in demand.

If you can also acquire some *arranging* skills, your potential earnings can increase substantially. Arrangers write out the parts that musicians play. This requires strong music reading and writing skills as well as a thorough understanding of the musical style(s) in which you are working. Arrangers are particularly valuable at recording sessions. The rental of a recording studio, added to the high per-hour cost of studio musicians, can easily amount to hundreds of dollars for each hour of time. A good arranger saves time and money by translating musical ideas into exact parts. If you feel that you have an arranger's ear, it might be wise to take some courses and develop the necessary techniques. Some musicians become so proficient at arranging that it becomes their primary career.

While the ability to arrange is always useful and potentially very profitable, the arrangements must be written in such a way that musicians can read them easily. Some arrangers do not have a neat handwriting or the time to write out professional-looking parts. They must employ the services of a *copyist,* who rewrites the parts from the arranger's original score sheets. Copying is a good part-time job for any musician with a neat handwriting. It is a particularly valuable experience for aspiring arrangers who want a firsthand look at how scores are put together.

If you want to seriously consider the kinds of skills a professional musician should have, do not look at the things your favorite superstars *can't* do. Instead, try to master as many skills as you can so that you will be competitive with all of the other highly qualified people who are trying to get ahead.

Try to play more than one instrument, if possible. Most saxophone players are also expected to double on clarinet and flute. Guitarists may be called upon to play electric, acoustic, or bass guitar. Drummers should be able to perform on all kinds of percussion instruments. Piano players are often asked to play organ or synthesizer. Remember, the more flexible and versatile you are, the better your chances for success.

Public Relations

In the relatively small circle of professional musicians, your reputation and contacts are extremely important. When you are starting your musical career, hang out at various clubs and recording studios in order to get to know people in your field. Try to get heard by anyone who might be in a position to help you find work. Make friends with people who play the same instrument as you. Perhaps they will have two offers for the same evening and ask you to fill in for them. Make sure you are dependable. Show up on time. Wear the appropriate kind of clothes. Bring any additional equipment that you might need. Invest a few dollars and print up business cards. Develop a written resume that lists your accomplishments. Remember, every musical situation is important, especially during the first few years of your career. People who hire you are not only interested in how well you play. They also want to know if you are dependable, flexible, and easy to work with.

Getting Organized and Taking Care of Business

Music professionals often make a point of saying that if you are going to make a living as a musician, you have to keep two words in mind—music and *business.* There are hundreds of excellent players and singers who do not succeed as professionals. Many of these people cannot cope with the constant business considerations with which today's musician must contend. He or she must know something about contracts and accounting just to get properly compensated for work. But this is just the beginning of the business side of a successful musician's work.

Phillip Namanworth is a talented New York-based studio musician and songwriter. He has worked with Roberta Flack, Ry Cooder, and many other well-known artists. Although he has been making a good living for a number of years, Phillip has only recently concentrated his energies on the business side of his music.

> I used to live from day to day without any kind of a plan or program. I was making money but I ran up a lot of debts because I didn't keep track of how I spent it. Now I look at my life as a business. I decided to structure my life by thinking of myself as being in my own business. I'm in the business of Phillip Namanworth Enterprises. . . . That means that I'm always doing something positive to improve my career. If there's no work coming in, I'm on the phone calling people and trying to generate work. . . . I've been studying the things that successful people do in any business and trying to follow their lead.

Phillip Namanworth observes that there is no way for aspiring musicians to get the kind of training that will prepare them for the rigors of a freelance lifestyle. There are many cases of talented people making lots of money who cannot seem to organize their lives. In order to be truly successful, musicians must somehow find a balance between the creative and the business sides of their careers. Phillip continues:

> When I was younger, I worked a lot. But I didn't know how to make the best use of what I had going for me. I had up and down periods, but I just couldn't put it all together. . . . Now I realize that I am in the business of being successful, and this has also helped me become more productive with my music. I find that fame and money help me take my music to a higher level. I need money so that I'm not always devoting all my time and energy to paying the rent. It's nice to make life into an adventure, and worrying about the rent isn't very exciting after awhile. But you need money in order to stop worrying about making money. . . .

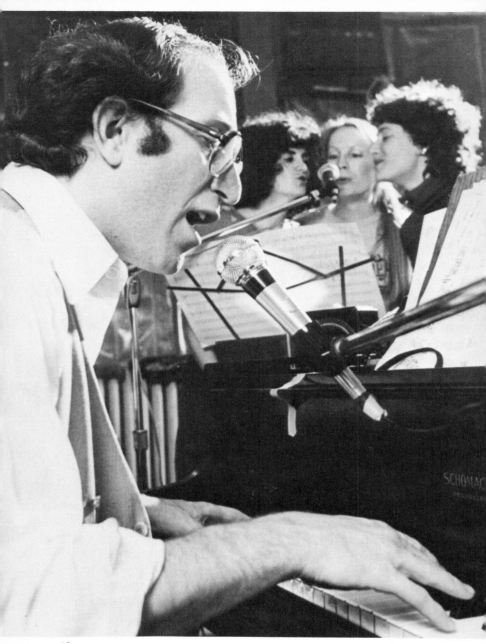

Phillip Namanworth plays one of his arrangements with background singers. (BOGERTMAN)

Even the most successful freelance musicians go through dry periods during which there is no work coming in. One key to surviving as a freelance person is using this time in a productive way. This might involve calling up established contacts to let them know you are available, developing new contacts, working on your environment, and organizing your papers and finances in a businesslike way. Phillip has found that utilizing time properly pays off.

> I try to structure my life as much as possible. I usually like to get up early and get right to work. But if I sleep late one day, it's because of a plan. Some people like to sleep late and work through the night. That's fine if you can still get your work done. But you must work out some kind of a schedule that allows you to be productive.
>
> I've found that an organized, well-structured lifestyle generates itself into the future. But living day-to-day doesn't really generate that much into the future. This holds true not only for musicians, but for any creative person involved with freelance work.

Life On the Road

Traveling is a reality for musicians at all levels of success. Many popular musicians spend the early years of their careers traveling around the country playing hit songs in a particular style—top-40, rhythm and blues, or country. Each member of such a road band usually earns between $300–500 a week, out of which he pays for lodging, food, and travel expenses. A year or two spent in a road band at this level will educate you in the realities of being a musician. These can include drunken audiences that throw bottles at the band, cars that break down in freezing weather and cost an entire week's salary to repair, and club owners who fire you after the first night because you are playing top-40 and they asked for a country band.

There are, of course, much better road jobs. A sideman with a top recording artist can easily earn $1,000 a week plus expenses. The travel arrangements and accommodations also tend to be a lot better at this level. But there are still drawbacks. It is not easy to finish working and then go back to a strange motel room in an unfamiliar city night after night. It takes a very dedicated and mature person to deal with the loneliness this kind of lifestyle demands. Most musicians eventually try to remain close to their homes as much as possible. But a few actually enjoy the traveling.

Saxophone player-singer Junior Walker has been on the road for the past twenty years. At one time, he was a top-name act on Motown Records and traveled first class. At this point in his career, he is still in demand. But the amount of money he makes dictates that he and his band travel by car and van instead of airplane.

"There's a line in one of my songs," Junior says. " 'I'm going to lead the life I love and love the life I lead.' That's how I feel about traveling around all the time. I just love going from place to place. Wouldn't you like to wake up in the morning, look out the window, and know that tomorrow you'll be waking up in another city?"

Becoming "Street Smart"

There are many situations that come up in a musician's life that can devastate a person who does not know how to deal with them. A booking might be canceled at the last minute. The drummer's car can break down on the way to the job. The bass player just got a much better offer and quit the band. At the end of a night's work, the club owner tries to pay you $100 less than the amount you agreed upon. Since the job came in at the last minute, there was no time to draw up a written contract. These are situations that all working musicians have to confront. The ability to deal with these setbacks can be at least as important as any kind of formal schooling. One can only handle situations as they come up. But if you intend to pursue a career as a professional musician, you had better be strong enough to deal with a variety of hassles.

Insiders will often refer to the music and entertainment business as a "cut-throat business" and a "scene loaded with money-grabbing hustlers." Many music business professionals point out that dirty dealing exists in other businesses as well. But the thing that makes the entertainment business unique is that the products being bought and sold are human beings.

There are some small-time hustlers looking to exploit hungry people with musical talent. But there are also many honest and reputable agents, managers, and club owners. The only rule for dealing with people in this business is to follow your instincts. You might need to get "burned" once or twice before you develop the right kind of instincts. But you should try to get all of your business agreements in writing. If you are hired to play at a club whose owner you do not know, ask for part of your money in advance. Remember, the world of popular music is an ocean that has lots of sharks. If you are going to be successful, you must learn to swim around them.

Education

Because the music business is so competitive and difficult, it might be wise to get a college education. You certainly do not need to be a music major in order to become a successful rock or country musician. However, you might want to develop skills in another area so that you will have something to fall back on. Music education used to be a convenient related course of study. But jobs have now become scarce in this area too. Perhaps the aspiring musician would benefit most from a course of college study that would include business, law, and psychology in addition to some relevant music electives.

People with a burning desire to enter the music business sometimes feel that they are better off pursuing their goal immediately after high school. There is no one right answer. You will never fail an audition because you lack a college degree. But, on the other hand, the course work and the years you spend in college may help you develop the maturity and nonmusical skills that one needs to make a successful and fulfilling career as a musician.

Genya Ravan, a well-respected rock vocalist who has been singing professionally for twenty years, believes that the best schooling for a young musician is to get out on the road and play. She herself has spent many years as a traveling musician. In the early sixties she was with an all-girl group called Goldie and the Gingerbreads. Later she was the leader of an all-male band called Ten Wheel Drive. In recent years, Genya has recorded two solo albums—*Urban Desire* and *And I Mean It.* Today, she is the co-owner of Polish Records and one of the very few female record producers in the business. Her entire musical education comes from living and working in music.

You've got to go through the pitfalls in order to learn this business. Some people call this "paying dues," but I think of it as "schooling." The experiences of dealing with musicians, business people, and audiences is what this business is all about. If you sign a bad contract and get burned, you can only blame yourself. Next time, go out and get a good lawyer. But as far as bombing in front of audiences and dealing with other people in the band, that's school.

Pleasing the Crowd

Most people who become popular musicians want to communicate to their audiences. A classical or jazz composer might write something with the understanding that the public might not be able to appreciate their work for many years. But popular musicians and singers must realize that audience response is an important ingredient in the formula for success at any level. If you are working small clubs, you will soon be fired if people do not show up and applaud your music. Many club owners want people to dance so that they will become thirsty and order drinks. If the music your band plays is not good for dancing and enough drinks do not get sold, you will be replaced. If you are one of the few bands lucky enough to get a record contract, that record had better sell or the company will drop you like a hot potato.

Performers come to understand that audiences do not always respond in terms of how good the music sounds. If a crowd is in a good mood, they will applaud for almost anything that is loud and fast. If, for some reason, an audience is not feeling especially receptive, it can be very hard for a band to get through to them. But all professionals must learn how to deal with this very tough part of the business.

"There's no real trick to performing," claims Genya Ravan. "You can't get down on an audience just because they're not getting into the music at the beginning of a set. Sometimes they won't respond until the middle or end of a set. When I perform, I always pick one person in the audience who is responding and direct my singing only to him. That's how I keep myself going with a bad audience. If you can maintain that contact with even one person, eventually the rest of the audience will get into it."

Working with other Musicians

More than almost any other kind of work, the success of a musician depends on the efforts and abilities of others. The greatest rock music has been made by bands rather than individual performers. But bands tend to break up eventually for a number of reasons. While you do want to build strong and lasting relationships with other players and singers, you should try not to become dependent on anyone but yourself. If you are a member of a band that is starving and suddenly you get an offer to work, you must weigh your decision very carefully. Perhaps your current band is just about to have a breakthrough. Would it be wise to leave in order to accept a short-term job with another group? Every situation warrants its own decision. But you would do well to weigh your potential as an individual musician against the commitment you make to any group.

When you join a new group, be sure to find out what your interest is in the earnings and expenses. If part of your earnings are being deducted to pay for advertising, equipment, and other expenses, you are entitled to a larger share. If your involvement is strictly as a sideman, you should be paid a set fee on a per-job or per-week basis. Do not believe any bandleader or manager who does not want to pay you now and promises you will be rewarded after the group has a hit record. Try to get all of your business agreements in writing, especially on long-term projects. This is not a sign of distrust, but a standard procedure for professionals.

It is essential for bands to keep personal disagreements out of their music. All people who work closely are bound to have arguments. When a group is on the road, the pressures of working as well as living together can mount up. But as a professional musician, it is up to you to make sure that any and all personal differences are left behind before you hit the stage.

"When I was with Goldie and the Gingerbreads, we often had terrible fights right before we went on to perform," Genya Ravan recalls. "But the music was so good that we would hug each other at the end of the set and forget all about the fights. After awhile, we really couldn't stand each other. But if audiences love your music and go crazy whenever you play, how can you stay mad?"

Studio Work

Some of the best paying jobs for a freelance musician are in recording studios. Although there are hundreds of studios all over America, the majority of the work is in the three major music business cities—New York, Los Angeles, and Nashville. There are about ten "first-call" singers and musicians on each instrument who do the bulk of the better studio jobs. Normal compensation for studio work is about $50 an hour. But the "heaviest" musicians can just about name their price. Some demand $1,000 a session, regardless of its length.

It is extremely difficult to break into the first-call category. But if you are a talented and versatile musician, you might be able to earn part of your income as a studio musician. Record dates, commercials, movies, and television soundtracks are the most common opportunities for studio work. The *client* who hires the musicians can be a record company, an independent producer, an advertising agency, or a film company. The actual hiring is done by *contractors* who have a book of proven singers and musicians. Many contractors are musicians themselves who are skilled in recruiting the right players for particular situations. Here is how most studio dates are organized:

The client will call up a producer or arranger and explain

the requirements of the date. The producer or arranger might have certain musicians he is familiar with and call them first. More commonly, a contractor is called and asked to "book the date." The producer or arranger may request particular players or singers as their first choice. If they are not available, the contractor will suggest a second choice. Sometimes the contractor will ask a musician to recommend someone else who can fill his shoes. That is why young musicians should get to know the top people on their instrument. If you can make a good impression on one or two established players, they may direct some work your way. But again, timing, luck, and public relations skills are as essential as musical talent.

A competent studio musician must learn to work well in a variety of situations. Sometimes the client or producer may not be able to express his musical wishes, and it is up to the musician to try to come up with an appropriate part. On other occasions, a musician might have an idea of how to improve a written arrangement. Some producers and arrangers welcome creative input from musicians. Others insist that the part be played exactly as written. If you are going to be a successful studio musician or singer, you must place the wishes of those paying for the session before your own personal tastes. If you can become sensitive to the needs of different clients and develop the musical skills to give them what they are looking for, you might be able to build a full-time or lucrative part-time career as a studio musician.

Getting a Record Deal

Even the best and most successful studio players and singers get tired of customizing their music to the needs of others. Most musicians start out with a desire to express themselves and win acceptance for their own particular musical statement. That is why every musician wants to get recorded—not just as a sideman on somebody else's record, but as a recording artist in his own right.

If you can somehow become one of the few musicians to break into the very closed circle of successful recording artists, you can make spectacular sums of money. But while you are trying to break in, you might find yourself in a situation in which you are earning no money. Most record companies are only interested in artists with original songs. There are very few paying jobs for unsigned bands who play their own music. In places like New York, groups sometimes pay club owners for the privilege of exposing their music, on the off-chance that a big-time manager or record executive might be in the audience.

Many bands who start out playing current hits in a particular style and then try to make their mark as recording artists playing original music suddenly find themselves without an income.

"When my group was playing top-40 tunes at clubs and Air Force bases," Genya Ravan recalls, "I used to come home with enough money to buy a car. But as soon as we started making records, we were broke.... At one point, we were even close to having a hit single. But it's hard for any group to last when you're starving to death."

There are some bands that start out with the sole intention of getting a record contract. These groups are often built around the talents of one or more *singer-songwriters.* Because these bands do all of their own writing, singing, and playing, they are called *self-contained bands.*

The model for most self-contained bands is the Beatles. They were the first major group to do it all themselves. Before the Beatles, most successful performers did not write or even choose the songs they recorded. But since the late sixties, most record companies will only sign artists who do their own writing. There are two basic steps that a band

Genya Ravan singing with Ten Wheel Drive. (COURTESY OF RECORD WORLD MAGAZINE)

has to go through in order to be in a position to get a record contract. They must make a demonstration tape (demo) of their best songs. They must be ready to perform live (showcase) for the companies that like what they hear on the demo.

The Demo

Back in the 1950's, musicians made demos in their garages that were sometimes released by record companies. Today's recording technology is so advanced that even the most sophisticated demos are rarely released as finished records. Record company executives will insist that a band does not have to spend a great deal of money to make a good demo. But when record company people listen to a demo, it is difficult not to compare what they are hearing to finished records that are played on the radio. This means that a band should submit something that is closer to a finished product than it is to just a rough indication of what they can do. Record executives will claim that they can "hear past" a poorly recorded demo, but many of them cannot.

Even if a band spends thousands of dollars and makes a great demo, they will probably not get a fair hearing at most record companies unless the demo is sent to the company by somebody with clout. Who has clout in the music business? Radio disc jockeys, managers, agents, entertainment lawyers, established stars, and other people with status in some phase of the music business. If a person with enough clout sends your demo into a record company, you can be reasonably sure that it will get heard.

As a rule, a band that does not have a well-known manager would do well to employ the services of a reputable New York- or Los Angeles-based music business attorney. These services do not come cheaply. But you will be throwing out your money on a demo if you cannot eventually get it heard by the right ears. Lawyers are not as beseiged with tapes as managers and record companies, and they do wield tremendous power in the business. If a powerful lawyer calls up a record executive and says, "I'm sending up a tape of a new group," that executive will listen to it. But if *you* mail your demo to that same executive, you will probably get it returned unopened.

The Showcase

If you are an unsigned group that plays only original material, it is not likely that you can work regularly, especially in major music business centers like New York, Los Angeles, and Nashville. There are some record companies that will dispatch somebody to hear a band in another part of the country if that group has attracted attention from local radio stations or other sources. But this is the exception rather than the rule. Many performers move to one of the major centers in order to be close to where the important music business people are. It stands to reason that a record executive would be more willing to audition a promising group at a club or rehearsal studio in the same city. But aspiring recording artists should always be prepared to get "stood up" when they are showcasing.

Roger Probert is an A&R (artist and repertoire) executive for Atlantic Records. Part of his job is finding and signing new talent for the label. As a former musician, he went through many evenings waiting for record company executives to audition his group.

> I found that A&R people didn't show up to my showcases about 90 percent of the time. Most musicians think record executives are the plague of the earth and I used to feel the same way. But there are sometimes legitimate reasons for an executive to miss a pre-arranged audition.

I might have an appointment to audition a band at 7 P.M. that evening. Their manager will usually call the same morning to confirm that I'll be there. But if one of the acts I've already signed to the label has a major catastrophe, I've got to take care of that. And if the president of my company suddenly calls and asks me to fly to Ohio because there's a hot new act that another label is about to sign, I've got to go there instead of to the showcase. . . . I know of some A&R people who stand bands up if there's a ball game on television that they want to watch. I would never do anything like that, but there are times that I am forced to cancel out.

Contacts and Clout

The importance of establishing the right contacts can never be overestimated in the record business. No matter how great your talent is, you will not get ahead unless it is brought to the attention of the right people. The resource section at the end of this chapter will direct you to several books that list important managers, attorneys, and song publishers in the music business. Even if you live outside of one of the major centers, you can still establish important connections by phone or mail. Attorney Seymour Feig has helped many new performers find record contracts. He offers the following suggestions:

Establish a cult following in your local area. Play all of the clubs and make sure you publicize your appearances. Try to play good and original music. Be commercial, but don't sound like anyone else. Stay away from phony managers who sign groups to awful contracts. They put up a little bit of money and then ask for your life's blood in return. Try to find a legitimate manager, a good music business lawyer, or some other person with musical contacts. . . . I'll try to help make a deal for an unknown group. If I think they're talented enough, I might even work out some kind of deferred payment plan. I enjoy helping young people. If I can make a record deal for a new artist, I feel ten feet tall.

Dealing with Rejection

Even if you make the greatest demo, showcase for all the right people, and establish topnotch contacts, you still might not be able to get a record deal in today's tight market. Perhaps the kind of music your group is playing is a little ahead of its time. Or perhaps another musical style is in vogue at the moment your group comes to a record company's attention. Seymour Feig feels that A&R people are often more concerned with short-term trends than overall musical quality.

> Too many A&R people tend to be lawyers and accountants rather than men of music. Years ago, an A&R man came from the ranks of musicians, engineers, or producers, so he could listen intelligently. Today you've got a lot of guys listening who have dull ears. They're afraid to set trends so they follow trends. Many record companies find people who know only rock or only disco. . . . They should try to sign a variety of talented artists in all musical styles in order to build a greater market.

Unfortunately, record deals can fall through not only because of trends, but for many other reasons which are completely out of the musician's control. There are also dozens of fine groups who land record contracts and get dropped from the label when the record does not sell. There can be a hundred reasons for a record not selling. But the results are usually the same. Record companies will rarely risk making a second album if the first one flops.

There are only a few performers who have made it to the top without going through long periods of disappointment or rejection. Phillip Namanworth expresses the sentiments of most experienced musicians when he says, "Music is a business full of rejection, and you've really got to get strong if you're going to hang in there. You'd better be able to take a punch because some people are going to tell you that your work is awful. Others won't even return your tape after they've rejected it. So you had better fortify yourself and be able to deal with that kind of thing."

Mark Schimmel has been trying to get a record deal for his current band for over a year. He has been in New York for seven years, knocking on doors and trying to get signed as a singer-songwriter. His present band—Trouble-maker—has stirred up some interest among record companies. They have performed at some of the best rock clubs in the city and have even gotten paid for their efforts. Mark considers this "a feat similar to performing open-heart surgery, because club owners almost never pay unsigned original groups."

At this time, Mark appears to have all the tools. A tight band, a good demo, a well-known record producer, an experienced, hard-working manager, and something he calls "the killer instinct." Mark feels that many talented musicians quit too soon because they can not take the disappointments and rejections after awhile. He believes that a serious performer should allow himself at least ten years before throwing in the towel. Mark is determined to see things through no matter what transpires.

> If this band breaks up, I'll get other musicians. If my producer leaves—which he will have to do eventually if we don't get a record deal—I'll find myself another producer. After spending so many years getting my craft down, I'm ready to do whatever it takes and not crumble under the pressure. In order to develop that type of an attitude, I've had to adopt a kind of killer instinct. That doesn't mean that I'm going to hurt

anybody, but I don't plan to let this business crush me as it does so many musicians.

Mark has the following advice for young people who want to make it in this tough career: "Keep forging ahead with your music, but don't forsake your personal lifestyle. Get a manager to wave your flag for you. If you can't get anybody other than yourself interested in what you're doing, that might be a sign that you need to change your act. Formulate a plan and don't be afraid to stick it out. There really aren't that many secure jobs around anyway. You might be better off going after the thing you really want instead of conforming to what other people expect you to do."

Financial Considerations

Before a group ever makes a nickel from a record deal, the record company must first recoup all the money spent in the process of making that record. This includes advances to musicians and producers, studio costs, promotion and publicity costs, and any other costs that have anything to do with the recording artists. Seymour Feig estimates that a record company starts making money after an album has sold about 20,000 copies. But since the average first-album artist usually receives a 5 percent royalty, he would not be entitled to any money until many times that number of albums has been sold. This means that most groups make no money from records for the first two or three years of their contract unless they have a top-ten record.

Now let's look at what it costs a bandleader like Mark Schimmel to get his group into a position of having a reasonable "shot" at landing a record contract. Keep in mind that the group's manager, Niles Siegel, has invested an even greater sum into Troublemaker.

Mark Schimmel (center) and Troublemaker showcasing at Trax in New York City. (FRED DEVAN)

Troublemaker had nine jobs in 1981, which earned them a total of $1,800. Every time the group traveled to a job, they rented a van for $100 to haul their equipment. When a group works at a top club, it is important that they carry their own sound man and someone to help set up and tear down the equipment (roadie). This costs another $100 per job. These two expenses alone used up the band's entire fee for the night.

The rental of a good rehearsal hall in New York costs $15 an hour, $45 for a three-hour rehearsal. Troublemaker only rehearses once a week now. But when the group first got together, they rehearsed three times a week. Mark's share of these expenses came to $2,200. Because Mark is the leader and main singer-songwriter, he did not get paid on any of the jobs. Since the four other band members have much less to gain if a record contract comes through, Mark promised to pay them something for every job they worked. This cost him another $500. Because Mark lives in New York and the rest of the band members live in New Jersey, all of his calls to them were long distance. His phone bill for the year—$1,000. Although the group's manager raised the money for their demos, Mark decided to make some improvements on his own at a cost of $800. Equipment, repairs, and clothing came to another $1,100. Here's a summary of Mark's out-of-pocket expenses for 1981:

Rehearsal halls	$2,200
Studio Costs	800
Payments to band members	500
Telephone	1,000
Clothing	400
Equipment	400
Repairs and Accessories	150
Taxis to rehearsals	725
	$6,175

SONGWRITER

Perhaps the quickest and least expensive way for a person to break into the popular music field is through songwriting. There is lots of competition, and it would be going too far to claim that the field is wide open. But good songs are always in demand. Charles Koppelman is president of the Entertainment Company, an organization that publishes songs and produces records for artists like Barbra Streisand, Janis Ian, and Glen Campbell. Koppelman usually tries to discourage young performers who seek to enter the popular music field. But he feels that the prospects are much better for aspiring songwriters.

> A talented songwriter has the easiest road to hoe in this business. . . . Like any other source material, good songs are hard to find. The song is the root and the most important ingredient in creating a hit. In a movie you need a good script, and in the music business, the song is like the script. That's what draws the listener in and allows him to relate to what the artist is singing.

The Entertainment Company generates material for its artists by purchasing catalogues of songs from other publishers and maintaining a staff of writers. Because of the top performers who are signed to the company, new writers are constantly trying to get their songs heard by Mr. Koppelman and his staff. With all of this input, the Entertainment Company is always on the lookout for new hit songs and people who can write them.

> You have to look hard to come up with that special three or four minute thing that captures a listener's attention. In a film, you have two hours to win over an audience. But with songs,

you have three and a half minutes to give the listener something original that he is going to want to hear over and over again.

Breaking into the Field

The first thing a songwriter must do to get his or her work heard is to make a demo that presents the songs in a way that communicates to the person listening. You do not need to spend hundreds of dollars to make an effective demo. What you do need is a simple presentation of the song by a good singer accompanied by guitar or piano. If you have your own group and some adequate home taping equipment, that's fine too. Try to put no more than three or four songs on each tape. Try to put songs of a similar style on the same tape, so that the listener does not get confused. Always put your best song first. If the listener is not attracted to your first offering, he probably will not listen to the rest of the tape.

Find the names and addresses of publishers who are interested in the kind of songs you are writing. Find out the name of a particular person at one of the companies and send your tapes to that person. You can find this information by reading the music business trade weeklies—*Billboard, Cashbox,* and *Record World.*

If you are concerned about your work being "ripped off" by someone who hears your tape, you can copyright your songs. Most reputable publishers do not engage in such practices. But you still might want to protect yourself. For information on copyright laws and procedures, write to the U.S. Copyright Office at the Library of Congress in Washington, D.C.

If you can get somebody with clout interested in your songs, you might want to let that person "run" with them. As in securing a record deal, the first step of getting a fair listening is crucial. If a reputable manager or music business lawyer wants to show your songs to publishers, they can often pick up the phone and speak to the right person at the right publishing company for your work. It is more likely that your tape will get heard than if you mail it yourself. Even if the company is not interested, you may get a response explaining why your work is rejected and some constructive criticism.

For those writers who would rather do the work themselves, Charles Koppelman advises that delivering a tape in person is likely to produce better results than sending it through the mail. "Save enough money to go to a major music center," he counsels. "Pound the pavement and knock on the door of every good music publisher. . . . We always listen to songs that are sent here. . . . But we are more apt to listen if you drop it off in person and say that you are coming to pick it up tomorrow. If my assistant tells me that someone from Cleveland dropped off a tape and he's coming back to pick it up, I'll try to listen to it right away because I know that it will be gone in the morning. But if it arrives by mail, it can sit here for six months before anyone listens to it."

There are two other ways of breaking in as a songwriter—songwriting contests and "vanity" publishing houses. There are a number of nationwide and local songwriting contests that are open to anyone who cares to enter. The winners of these contests get their work heard and sometimes get signed by publishers. The music trade papers and magazines like *Rolling Stone* carry information about the various contests. There is usually a small entrance fee, but it is well worth the expense if you really believe in your songs.

Do not enter into any kind of songwriting agreement where you are asked to put up money in order to get published. There are a number of "vanity" publishing companies that will publish any song for a fee. These firms generally have no interest in the quality or style of what they publish. Most reputable publishers make their money by getting your song to record companies and managers who can place them with recording artists. But vanity publishers rarely try to place songs. They are aware that people who are hungry to enter the music business will be easy marks. If you have any doubts about a publisher, check with your local Better Business Bureau. But the rule of thumb is that *publishers pay writers*, not the other way around.

Education and Training

The ability to write popular songs is largely a natural talent. Although some songwriters are accomplished musicians, a number of successful people have written hit songs without any apparent musical background. This is particularly true of people who write lyrics. Sandy Linzer is one example of a hit songwriter who had no musical training or background. "I was hanging around with a friend of mine who was running a few things down on the guitar," he recalls. "I said, 'Hey, I think I hear some lyrics for what you're playing.' That was the beginning of my songwriting career. Before that, I never had any involvement with music, nor had I given any thought to becoming a songwriter."

Within a few short months, Sandy Linzer was co-writing hits for the Four Seasons. From his early successes, Sandy has built a solid career as a songwriter and record producer. There have been similar stories of lyric writers who were lucky enough to hook up with the right composer. Though people who write the music for songs tend to have more training and background, the hardest thing to find is a good lyric writer. If you think you might be good at writing words for songs, try to find a musician who will work with you. But if you plan to build a career in songwriting, you should try to acquire some facility on the piano or the guitar. If you plan to approach songwriting from the point of view of music rather than words, you would do well to master as many musical styles as you can.

There are a few songwriting workshops that you may want to look into. But the main training for a songwriter is to sit down and start turning out tunes. You can work alone or with one or more partners. At the beginning, you should experiment with as many styles and as many co-writers as you can. Compare your stuff to the tunes that are being played on the radio and try to be self-critical. You may have to write a hundred or more songs before you come up with something that you feel is good enough to send around to publishers. But if you can get your song recorded, all of your efforts will have paid off.

Lifestyle

"Being a songwriter is a total way of life," says Doug Frank, who has written for Dionne Warwick, Cissy Houston, and The Spinners.

You can get ideas for songs at any time. If I'm eating dinner and somebody says, "I like your shoes," I might write that down to use in a song. I always carry a pad and pen with me because I'm always looking for titles and new concepts.

If you want to be a writer, you'd better be prepared to dive in head first, because there is no other way. Your personal relationships better be with someone in the music business or someone who is extremely understanding. Songwriters must come and go as they please because there are no set hours or routines. . . . If I have to be in the recording studio at three in the morning to work on a project, that's the way it has got to be. You sometimes find that you neglect other aspects of your life because you become so overwhelmed by the music business.

Jeanne Napoli is Doug's current writing partner. After spending years as a nightclub performer, Jeanne has become a skilled songwriter. She believes that many singers eventually try their hand at writing songs. She finds that the two careers require very different kinds of discipline.

> I find that performing takes a much more rigorous kind of discipline than songwriting. You don't just sit down and say, "I'm going to write a song." I don't write every night. I write whenever the inspiration hits me. . . . I like to have the freedom to go out and touch the world. I get a lot of my inspiration from just hanging out with different people.

Experienced writers often try to vary their activities so that they can stay fresh. While they are generating new songs, writers are also perfecting tunes that are in various states of completion. They also do what they can to get recording artists to hear their work.

"I find there is something else to do every day," says Doug Frank. "If we're not working on new songs, we're in the studio finishing up things we've already written. We also spend time making tape copies, seeing people, and typing letters. We probably do just as much leg work trying to sell our songs as our publishing company. But I consider all of that part of the job."

Most people who make their living as songwriters thoroughly enjoy their work. They look at songwriting as their lives rather than just their work. The struggling songwriter who never gets his or her work recorded may have to deal with the anxiety of wondering if the work is worthy. But in a field like this, success breeds success. If you

Songwriters Doug Frank and Jeanne Napoli collaborating on a
tune.

know that people are going to hear your work on the radio,
it inspires you to write more and better songs.

"Every once in awhile, I remember how lucky I am to be
doing very well in a business where I can do what I love to
do," says Doug Frank. "Most people hate their jobs and
spend a whole year looking forward to their two-week vacation."

"We never think about a vacation," Jeanne adds, "because we're always on one."

Financial Considerations

Songwriting is a field in which a fortune can be made. But unlike performing, there are few paying situations for a young person starting out. The only way to make money as a songwriter is to get your songs recorded. Once that happens, you earn *royalties* from the sale of records and sheet music and from performances on the radio, television, or at concerts. A songwriter's royalties are collected by three performing rights organizations—ASCAP, BMI, and SESAC (see page 93). All published songwriters must belong to one of these organizations in order to collect money. All three organizations participate in programs and workshops for new writers. It would be a good idea to write to all three of them to find out how their services might benefit your career.

The big money in songwriting comes from having top-ten hits that get re-recorded (covered) by many artists. A song like Lennon and McCartney's "Yesterday," for example, has been covered hundreds of times. Any time a version of this song is performed, the writers earn money. All songwriters aspire to place their tunes with big name recording artists so that their work will be performed often and covered many times. A few years ago, many older songs were re-recorded as disco records. The writers of these songs found themselves collecting more money than when the songs originally became hits. That is the beauty of songwriting. Once your song gets known, it is likely to get recorded many times. Though your work has been long completed, you still collect royalties.

If, after you send your demo around, you get a favorable response from a publisher, there are a few important things to keep in mind:

- You must join one of the three performing rights organizations in order to collect any royalties. All three have their advantages. Check with your publisher and attorney to find out which is best for you.
- The American Guild of Authors and Composers (AGAC) is an organization that is dedicated to protecting the rights of songwriters. They have a standard contract which a writer and publisher can sign. The AGAC contract affords good protection to songwriters, although not all publishers will accept it. (See p. 94 for more information on AGAC.)
- If you are a singer-songwriter who is looking for a record deal and a record company is only interested in one of your songs, you would probably be wise to let them have it. Some singer-songwriters insist on recording their own work. But if you can get your song out by a major artist, your own performing career prospects will be much brighter. And don't forget those nice royalty checks.
- A songwriting contract is a complex matter. If you are working with a publisher on a per-song basis, an AGAC ageement will give you all the protection you need. But if the publisher asks you to sign a long-term agreement, you will need the council of a good music business lawyer.

MUSIC BUSINESS CAREERS

Record Producer

Producers are key people in both the creative and business aspects of making a record. Like the director of a movie, record producers control the pace and content of recording sessions. Few people start out with the intention of becoming record producers. Most begin their careers as musicians, songwriters, arrangers, or engineers. All producers have different strengths and weaknesses. But the successful ones have a number of things in common. In his book, *Producing Hit Records*, producer Dennis Lambert cites these five skills as essential for success in this career:

FACT SHEET
WRITING & ARRANGING CAREERS IN POPULAR MUSIC

Career	Opportuni- ties for Employment	Education and Training	Skills and Personality Traits
SONG- WRITER (Composer and/or lyri- cist)	1• Staff writer for publishing company 2• Commercial (jingle) song- writer for ad- vertising agency 3• T.V. and movie sound- tracks 4• Freelance	• No formal degrees re- quired • Knowledge of music nec- essary for composers, helpful for lyricist	• Knowledge and feel of the musical style(s) in which you are working • Business and public relations skills • Self-discipline • Versatility • A feel for cur- rent trends
ARRANGER	1• Record ses- sions 2• Movie and T.V. sound- tracks 3• Shows 4• Television	• College or conservatory education helpful • Courses in music theory and orchestra- tion	• Fluency in reading and writing instru- mental and vocal parts • Knowledge of musical styles • Ability to translate musi- cal ideas onto paper • Knowledge of current trends in music • Business and public relations skills

* Figures are approx. AMF scale—Local 802 (1981).

• The ability to pick hit artists and hit songs
• A feel for current trends
• A knowledge of the workings of the record business

Lifestyle	Earnings	Employment Outlook
• No regular hours • Night and week-end work • Little or no job security	1• Approx. $150 and up per week 2• Variable fee per session depending on track record plus residuals 3• and 4• Advance against royalties from performances, record and sheet music sales (royalties collected by BMI, ASCAP, and SESAC)	• Highly competitive but opportunities there for talented people who can get their work heard
• No regular hours • Must work under pressure of deadlines • Some night and weekend work	• Approx. $12 per ten line page (4 measures on a line) • Many arrangers charge a flat rate per song of approx. $200 to $500	• Very competitive

- The ability to present new artists and songs to the right people at record companies
- The ability to deal effectively with recording studio and record company personnel

These skills must be coupled with some technique in the art of making records. Many of our finest record producers began as arrangers or recording engineers. Others start out with few skills, save the ability to hire qualified people to take care of each phase of the recording process. These producers are basically contractors who know how to put the right combinations of talent together.

Producer-songwriter Sandy Linzer admits that when he started producing records he was little more than a contractor who knew how to pick people who got the job done. He still cannot read music or engineer a session on his own. But he is effective because of his good musical instincts and a general accumulation of knowledge which he has gained through experience.

> I don't write or read music. But I can hum the things I want people to sing and play. . . . I started producing out of necessity, because nobody else would put up the money to produce some of my songs. So I found the money myself and hired the people who would make the session work. At that point, I was little more than a contractor. Now I consider myself a successful producer who can handle any situation.

At this writing, Sandy Linzer has produced some forty records. His hits include "Lover's Concerto" by the Toys, "Brandy" by Looking Glass, and a recent album by T. S. Monk. He would prefer to devote more of his time to songwriting and let others handle the difficult chores of producing. But he has found that producing records gives him greater control over the presentation of his songs and a significant source of income.

A handful of top producers receive hundreds of thousands of dollars as an advance against royalties for working on an album. In such cases, the record company is relatively certain that the advance will be paid back by healthy record sales. Most of the top producers work independently. They are not affiliated with any particular record company and can select the projects they want to work on. There are also *staff producers* who are employees of a record company. They get paid a salary as well as a small royalty fee for every record sold.

Many of the major record companies are leaning toward independent rather than staff producers. They find it more desirable to hire name people as they need them and maintain smaller in-house staffs. This has created a situation where producers are paid in accordance with how "strong" or "hungry" they are. A strong producer with a track record of recent hits can almost name his price. A producer who has been off the hit parade for awhile will have to settle for a much lower fee.

Breaking In

Twenty years ago, a new producer could make a hit record for a few hundred dollars, sell it to a record company, and be off and running. Today, people spend thousands of dollars for demos. The cost of a completed master (finished record) is prohibitive. Still, an aspiring producer can break in if he or she *finds a good group, makes a presentable demo,* and *signs the group to an exclusive contract.*

Even if you are a potential giant in the producing field, most record companies will ignore you if you have no track record. Still, if you discover the next Beatles or Elton John, they may be forced to take notice. Unless you sign your singer or group to an exclusive production agreement, the record company will phase you out of the picture in favor of someone more experienced. Even with a binding contract, you may have to give up part of your interest in order to obtain a major record deal. But at least you will have to be paid back for your investment and given some piece of the deal.

If you are looking to strike out as an independent producer, get a good music business lawyer immediately. He will see to it that your contracts are binding, and his name and reputation will make you look stronger in the eyes of record executives.

Developing the Skills

There are a number of schools and colleges that give courses in record production, though most professionals do not value this training very highly. The best kind of training is to get familiar with the workings of a recording studio from any vantage point and to develop a knowledge of the music business.

"One of the keys to getting ahead in the production business is to get a job with an established, reputable company as early as possible," counsels producer Dennis Lambert. "It can be a record or publishing company, a booking agency, a management office, or even a retail record store. But it's vitally important to be visible in some way to the industry, to see who's coming and going, and to learn the best and most inexpensive way possible [of doing things]— on the job."

Genya Ravan's road to becoming a producer was spending nine years as a recording artist. By studying the strengths and weaknesses of other producers, Genya has found that the ability to deal with people is just as important as musical and business skills.

There's an awful lot involved in being a good producer. You've got to know when to *take* and when to stop. You've got to do whatever you can to create the right atmosphere. You've got to be a psychologist and be sensitive to what people need.

Producer Genya Ravan in the control booth at a recording session.

FACT SHEET
CAREERS IN THE MUSIC BUSINESS

Career	Opportunities for Employment	Education and Training	Skills and Personality Traits
RECORD PRODUCER	• Staff producer for a record company • Independent producer	• No formal degree required • Broad college background helpful • Musical training helpful • Related technical training helpful • Most successful producers have training and/or experience in one or more related areas of the music business	• Ability to pick hit songs and hit artists • Knowledge of record business • A feel for current trends • Ability to deal with people in recording studios and record companies • Strong business and public relations skills
BOOKING AGENT	• Established agencies • Self-employed	• Major agencies require college degree for entry level positions • Courses in business and contract law desirable	• Business and public relations skills • Ability to deal with artists, managers, club owners, and record companies • An aggressive, outgoing personality • Ability to work under pressure • Salesmanship

Lifestyle	Earnings	Employment Outlook
• Long and irregular hours • Night and weekend work • Staff producers get company benefits and may have other corporate responsibilities • Independent producers choose who they work with; they are self-employed with no company benefits	• Approx. $300–$600 per week for staff producers plus royalties • Independent producers get variable fee depending on track record • Can go into high six-figure income at top of scale	• Extremely competitive
• Long and irregular hours • Night and weekend work • Total involvement in work needed for success	• Based on a percentage of the work you book (approx. 10%) • Highly variable depending on the quality and number of acts you book	• Some openings for those willing to start at the bottom of a major agency

FACT SHEET
CAREERS IN THE MUSIC BUSINESS

Career	Opportunities for Employment	Education and Training	Skills and Personality Traits
MANAGER	• Established management companies • Your own business	• No formal degrees required • Broad college background with courses in business recommended • Seminars or courses in arts management • Most successful managers have extensive previous experience in the music business	• Business and public relations skills • Aggressive and outgoing personality • Ability to run every phase of an artist's career • Knowledge of and contacts within every phase of the music business • Ability to work under pressure
MUSIC LAWYER	• Record companies • Music business law firms	• Four year college degree, plus degree from accredited law school • Courses and/or practical experience in some phase of the music business helpful	• Ability to negotiate • Thorough understanding of the music business • Ability to deal with both performers and business people

Sometimes I act like a joker, other times I'm dead serious. If the situation calls for it, I'll call the artist or engineer over to the side and talk with him calmly. Ten minutes later, I might find it necessary to yell at someone. But you've got to make sure that everyone is happy and doing his thing.

Lifestyle	Earnings	Employment Outlook
• Long and irregular hours • *Total involvement with work* • Night and weekend work • Socializing with people in all phases of the music business	• Receive approx. 20% of their artists' earnings • Highly variable depending on number of artists and their success	• Easy to break in on a local level • Very closed at the highest levels
• Long hours • Some night and weekend work • Some travel • Total involvement with work	• Established music law firms charge a minimum of $125 an hour • A top lawyer can make a high six-figure income	• Very small closed field • Very difficult to obtain first position • Opportunities at record companies might be better than at law firms

MANAGERS

Musicians and singers who work local clubs often get their jobs through an *agent*. The function of an agent is to book talent into a room for a price. Agents earn their living by taking between 10 and 20 percent of their client's earnings.

If a performer succeeds in signing a record contract, he or she will sign with a major agency such as William Morris or ICM. These larger agencies perform the same functions for their clients as the local agent who books small clubs. They find work for their acts.

Most major performers sign exclusive agreements with one of the big agencies. But the most important person handling the career of any performer is the personal manager. When an agent lines up a single night engagement or an entire tour for a client, he deals with the manager. In fact, the big agencies will not even sign a group or individual artist unless they know that there is a personal manager looking after them.

Tom Mattola is one of the most successful managers in the rock music business. His clients include Hall and Oates, Split Enz, and King Creole & the Coconuts. This is how he sees the role of a manager.

> A manager's most important function is to cater to the creative needs of his artist. I try to involve my artists only in creative decisions and insulate them from as much of the nonsense as possible. . . . As a manager, I negotiate record contracts, publishing deals with ASCAP and BMI, and agency deals so that my artists get bookings. . . . A good manager should have the ability and flexibility to deal with any facet of the music business, whether it be the most minute or the most important. . . . If I was an act requiring personal management, I would want to be represented by a person who understood all of my artistic needs and had the ability to translate that into the world of business. (He would have to be somebody) who could deal with all those facets in a real aggressive and competent way.

As somebody who started in the business as a musician, Tom Mattola has unique insight into the needs and problems of performers. He also has very highly developed musical tastes and will only get involved with performers he really believes in. "How can you sell an artist that you don't believe in yourself?" he asks. "As a manager, you are, in essence, the salesman for that artist. I find it impossible to sell and represent an artist I don't believe in."

Breaking into the Field

Anyone who finds a group and gets them to sign a contract can become a manager. Performers are often so desperate that they will sign with anyone who puts up some money. But signing performers and guiding their careers in a competent way are two completely different things. Tom Mattola feels that an unknown manager who hooks up with even the greatest new act will wind up on the short end of the stick unless he understands the realities of the business.

> A new manager should get a good music lawyer to draw up a contract which will insure him a certain percentage of the group. Then, he should be prepared to give part of his interest to an established manager. This way, he can still be involved and his investment will be protected. If he tries to see it through on his own, he will have to call his attorney for almost daily advice. And that's going to cost him a lot of money. So you have to pay the piper somewhere along the line. But I don't look at that as giving up your golden opportunity. That *is* your golden opportunity.

Tom Mattola offers the following advice to young people who want to break into the business:

> Go to one of the major music capitals, and get involved in any phase of the business you can, whether it's packing records or working in the mailroom of the William Morris Agency. Some of the people who work in that mailroom become agents, and many managers start out that way.... Somehow, you've

got to pay your dues in this business if you really plan to make it your life and do it correctly. Otherwise, your success will be limited no matter how great your opportunities.

Education and Training

Most managers agree that specific courses in arts management and the music business are less valuable than practical experience. But they do feel that a college education is important. "These days," Tom Mattola points out, "you need a college degree to even get a job in the William Morris Agency's mailroom."

Niles Siegel has built a career in the music business without the benefit of a college education. He started out as a photographer and moved into the promotion department of Elektra Records. After several years of working for record companies and with name bands like the Doors and the Atlanta Rhythm Section, Niles decided to become a full-time manager. He is currently managing an aspiring New York rock band called Troublemaker. Although he has gained his knowledge of the business through experience, he believes a broad college background is essential for most aspiring managers.

I was lucky to break into this business, because I was a photographer with some good connections. But that's no basis for a career. Anyone who wants to be a manager should get a degree from a good college. Get a good background in business. Learn about business law and how to read a contract. Learn how to be logical in business. Get an understanding of what money means and how it works. There are a lot of things that I learned on the streets that would have been a lot easier to learn in a classroom.

Lifestyle and Money

If you are the manager of a group that makes $10 million a year, your 20 percent share would come to $2 million. But the other side of the coin is the manager who is investing his personal funds, hoping that his group will make it. Niles Siegel has been energetically managing Troublemaker for two years. He hopes that a $50,000 record advance will materialize in the near future, though this is by no means a certainty. *If* this kind of a deal does come through, Niles's 20 percent share would come to ten thousand dollars. "That would only pay me back for part of the cash that I've spent," he points out. "My phone bills are over $300 a month from Troublemaker's business alone. There were times that a band member needed $100 to pay his rent. I had to lend it to him, even though my rent didn't get paid that month. I've already spent over ten thousand dollars and I'm not even taking into account all the time I've put in. . . .

"This is not a very practical business. It's a lot like horse racing, but that's what makes it exciting. You put up your ten grand and two years of your time and hope that you'll win. If you do, you never have to worry about money again. But let's face it, you don't get into this business unless you love to take chances."

Tom Mattola has probably made enough money to stop working if he wanted to, but that is the furthest thing from his mind. "I work seven days a week, twenty hours a day. My life is always business, even when I'm taking a vacation. This is a telephone business and I have phones in my car and in every room in my house. This business is my life, and that's the way I like it."

ENTERTAINMENT LAWYER

When you speak to people about getting ahead in the music business, they will always tell you that an important key is to get yourself a good lawyer. For better or for worse, aspiring musicians and performers often seem to be more concerned with finding a powerful attorney than improving themselves musically. Alan Grubman is a top music lawyer whose clients include Billy Joel, Hall and Oates, and many other big stars. He explains the tremendous power of lawyers in the music business this way:

> Most record deals are negotiated by lawyers. That's why lawyers have taken on an expanded role in this business. They have become power brokers by representing important people. This has given lawyers a tremendous amount of power with record companies. The more important people you represent, the heavier you get, and the more clients come to you.
>
> It has taken me many years to accomplish this. But there is no record executive in the world who won't pick up my phone call as soon as I call. That means if I'm representing somebody with real talent, he'll probably get that talent seen and heard by the right people. But if a talented person goes to somebody who doesn't have that power to get through to the people who can sign and develop talent, that talent may go unnoticed forever.

Breaking into the Field

Most entertainment law firms will not hire a young person right out of law school. "We need people who can jump in and start turning work out immediately," explains Alan Grubman. "I don't have the time to train new people. In fact, I don't even have time to breathe. The only thing anyone in this firm has time to do is to service clients."

Like Alan Grubman, attorney Seymour Feig is swamped with resumes from young lawyers who want to break into the field.

A lot of people want to get into this business, but there are very few job openings. Many people have even offered to work for nothing. But it would be unfair to have law school graduates come in here and do things for nothing. The best solution is probably some kind of summer internship program while they are still in law school. . . . This is not a business that you can learn very quickly. It's a very specialized field of the law. You must be able to deal with all kinds of organizations and unions. Some music lawyers only handle record deals and the like. But I handle movies, books, and other related areas. I find it fascinating to involve myself in every aspect of the entertainment field.

In spite of the tight job market, Seymour Feig would not discourage a talented young person who really wants to enter the field. "Everybody needs good people in any business. But you've got to evolve and grow into a position. Colleges and law schools should give more practical courses in the music business. There should be more training grounds for people who want to enter this field."

If you have your mind set on entering this relatively closed career, you may have to seek out your own training grounds. Learn as much about music and the music business as you can. Take a part-time job for a management company or a booking agency. Offer to handle the business affairs of a local band with whom you are friendly. Get a job as a goffer at a recording studio, a music publisher, or an entertainment law firm. Get involved with your college radio station or entertainment committee. Read the music trade papers and speak to people who can help you. You may first have to take a position in another area of the law. But if you develop good legal skills and a working knowledge of the music business, you might just be able to talk somebody into hiring you.

Money and Lifestyle

Entertainment law can be a very lucrative field. Most attorneys charge a minimum of $125 an hour for their services. The top people can command much higher fees as well as a percentage of their client's earnings. The most successful music business lawyers make hundreds of thousands of dollars each year.

The lifestyle of a music lawyer is not unlike that of a successful manager or music business executive. There is a great deal of time spent on the phone. The separation between business and social activities is minimal. Music lawyers often do a good deal of traveling from one music business center to another and abroad. The most successful attorneys spend little or no time in court. The bulk of their time is spent negotiating for their clients.

The telephone in Alan Grubman's Manhattan office never stops ringing. It is his lunch hour, and his secretary is holding most of his calls. But even as he eats his lunch and discusses his career, he is trying to get through to the president of a record company to take care of some pressing business on behalf of a client.

There is no master plan or pre-ordained right road to take in order to reach the top in this field. There are probably a hundred music lawyers and maybe five real superstars in the field. It's hard for me to pinpoint the reasons why I've reached that level of success in my career. On an hour-to-hour basis, I'm not really aware of what I have or haven't accomplished. I just chip away at every problem. . . . I'm likeable. I've got a good sense of humor. I'm sincere and honest with my clients and I work very hard. I've always had great instincts when it comes to dealing with people and I still base most of my major decisions on those instincts.

As in any profession, music law attracts different kinds of people. Some become negotiation specialists. Others are better at turning out legal work and running an office. But all successful people in this career have paid their dues in the music business. Even the best practitioner of general law will not be properly equipped to negotiate a record or publishing deal. A music business lawyer is a specialist in his or her field, whose entire working life revolves around music and other areas of the entertainment industry. If you are fortunate enough to build a successful career in this field, you will have landed in one of the most powerful and financially rewarding professions in the music business.

CONCERT PROMOTER

There have been a few cases of people who developed instant credibility in the music business by promoting rock concerts. Twenty years ago, Sid Bernstein was looking through a London newspaper and noticed that a group called the Beatles was the biggest thing in Europe. The group had still not made a breakthrough in the United States. In fact, Bernstein had never even heard of them. But when he found out that the Beatles were scheduled to appear on the "Ed Sullivan Show," Bernstein saw his chance to become a force in the concert promotion business.

Because he was friendly with the people who operate New York's Carnegie Hall, Bernstein was able to secure an open date for a reasonable price. He then called up the

Concert promoter Ray Reneri relaxing backstage.

Beatles' manager, Brian Epstein, and secured the band's services for that date. Again, the price for the Beatles' services was very reasonable because the band had not yet become a force on the American music scene. By the time the Beatles arrived here for their first American tour, they were the hottest performers in the business. An unknown Sid Bernstein had become the first concert promoter to book the group and establish a relationship with their manager.

Twenty years later, Bernstein's method is probably the best way for a new person to get noticed in the concert promotion field. Find an act *before* they hit big. Secure an appropriate concert facility and put the whole thing together. This means that you must raise the money to rent the facility and pay the group. You must also convince the act's management and the operators of the facility that you are capable of pulling the whole thing together.

Ray Reneri, who has promoted and produced many concerts, considers this field "the biggest gamble in the music business." He also points out that, "There are one or two promoters in every city who have a monopoly on all of the major acts. The agencies just won't deal with anybody else, and it's not a matter of money. I've had the money for a major act and an okay from the act and their manager. But the agencies always say, 'You can only go through whoever the major promoter is in a particular city.' "

Unless you have the foresight to anticipate the coming of the next Beatles, you must start out with smaller acts. Agencies are more likely to sell an unproven promoter a new act or one that is not currently in the limelight.

"In order to break in as a promoter, you need enough money to gamble on your first couple of shows," Ray Reneri points out. "You had better be prepared to take a loss because you've got so much going against you. The act may not show up, or there can be a snow storm or hurricane. The top acts sell out well before the concert, so the top promoters are hardly taking any risk at all. But the promoter of smaller concerts is taking a much greater chance."

Reneri believes that a promoter must pay his dues by proving himself to agents and managers over a period of time. "If you're constantly buying talent from agencies and managers all the time over a two or three year period, they might give you a shot at something bigger. But nobody starts out in this business by booking acts like Rod Stewart and the Bee Gees. This is a very complicated business that takes time to learn, and the competition is fierce."

Concert promoters become successful through the building of relationships with agents, managers, and promoters. Howard Stein, one of the top concert promoters in New York, admits that the competition for these favorable relationships makes promoting concerts a "cutthroat" business. "These relationships are the promoter's only tangible asset," he observes. "If they change, he's out of business."

Additional Sources for Information About Careers in Popular Music and the Music Business

NATIONAL ACADEMY OF RECORDING ARTS AND SCIENCES (NARAS)—4444 Riverside Drive, Burbank, California 91505

Sponsors lectures on the recording arts at colleges and universities. Offers scholarships in music and related fields.

NATIONAL MUSIC PUBLISHERS ASSOCIATION—110 E.59th Street, New York, New York 10022

AFRO-AMERICAN MUSIC OPPORTUNITIES ASSOCIATION—P.O. Box 662, Minneapolis, Minnesota 55440

COUNTRY MUSIC ASSOCIATION (CMA)—7 Music Circle North, Nashville, Tennessee 37203

AMERICAN GUILD OF ORGANISTS—630 5th Avenue, New York, New York 10020

Good source of information about church music.

NATIONAL ASSOCIATION OF JAZZ EDUCATORS—P.O. Box 724, Manhattan, Kansas 66502

Aside from encouraging the teaching of jazz on all levels of education, the association strives to promote jazz improvisation as a serious form of musical expression. It also publishes the *N.A.J.E. Educator.*

THE FREELANCE NETWORK—P.O. Box 149, Old Chelsea Station, New York, New York 10011

A good source of information and contacts for people pursuing freelance music careers.

Performing Rights Societies

THE AMERICAN SOCIETY OF COMPOSERS, AU-
THORS AND PUBLISHERS—1 Union Plaza, New York,
New York 10023

A nonprofit society of music writers and publishers repre-
senting virtually every musical style. Monitors the performances
of its members' works. Serves as a clearinghouse for the negotiations of licenses and the protection of performing rights. Publishes a variety of resource material including a quarterly publication, *A.S.C.A.P. Today.*

BROADCAST MUSIC INCORPORATED (BMI)—40 W.
57th Street, New York, New York 10019

The largest performing rights organization in America.
Offers scholarships for promising young musicians and composers. Publishes a quarterly magazine, *BMI: The Many Worlds
of Music,* which consists of articles about composers and general
music articles.

SESAC INCORPORATED—10 Columbus Circle, New York,
New York 10019

The smallest of the three performing rights associations.
Strongest in the areas of country and religious music. Currently
seeking to expand its horizons into other musical areas.

Unions and Guilds

AMERICAN FEDERATION OF MUSICIANS (AFM)—
1500 Broadway, New York, New York 10036

Consists of over 650 affiliated unions in the United States
and Canada.

AMERICAN GUILD OF VARIETY ARTISTS (AGVA)—
1540 Broadway, New York, New York 10036

Serves primarily popular singers.

AMERICAN GUILD OF AUTHORS AND COMPOSERS—40 W. 57th Street, New York, New York 10019
Helps protect business rights and interests of songwriters.

AMERICAN FEDERATION OF TELEVISION AND RADIO ARTISTS (AFTRA)—1350 Avenue of the Americas, New York, New York 10019

SCREEN ACTORS GUILD (SAG)—1500 Broadway, New York, New York 10019

Publications

CONTEMPORARY MUSIC ALMANAC—Edited by Ronald Zalkind, Schirmer Books—MacMillan Publishing Company, New York, New York.
An invaluable resource which includes information regarding getting started in the music business, music business contracts, listings of public relations firms, recording studios, managers, attorneys, and music business publications, etc.

BILLBOARD'S INTERNATIONAL BUYER'S GUIDE ANNUAL—9000 Sunset Boulevard, Los Angeles, California 90069
Offers a complete listing of associations, professional organizations, record companies, music publishers, etc.

Music Trade Magazines

BILLBOARD—9000 Sunset Boulevard, Los Angeles, California, 90069

CASHBOX—119 W. 57th Street, New York, New York 10019

RECORD WORLD—1700 Broadway, New York, New York 10019

THE FRIDAY MORNING QUARTERBACK—Cherry Hill Plaza, 1414 E. Marlton Avenue, Suite 505, Cherry Hill, New Jersey 08034

COLLEGE MEDIA JOURNAL (CMJ)—P.O. Box 258, Roslyn, New York 11576

CHAPTER 3

Careers in
Classical Music

PERFORMING AND COMPOSING CAREERS

"When we remember any civilization, we remember the
art that comes down as part of the continuous thread of that
civilization. That's why it's exciting to be part of it. And
that's why I like to think of classical music as more than
just show business." (Henry Fogel, orchestra manager of
the New York Philharmonic)

Almost every person you speak to in the classical field
has a genuine love and excitement for the art form.
Whether you're talking to managers, critics, or publicity
people, the men and women who make their living in classical music are passionate about symphonic music and
opera. Most of them have had formal music lessons when
they were young, and some started out with ambitions to
become performers and composers.

96

For an aspiring young musician, the classical field demands a most serious commitment. In fact, many professionals prefer to use the term *serious* music rather than classical music. It is a serious undertaking, indeed, to become a topnotch classical musician, even on the high school level. A member of New York City's All City Orchestra—a high school orchestra made up of the area's best young musicians—has already put in hundreds of hours of practice time. In spite of the talent and dedication of these young performers, most of them will not become full-time professionals.

We can draw a comparison between the talented high school musician and an outstanding young athlete. The best football player on his high school team has a good chance of getting a college scholarship. After that, he will be competing with other athletes who were all the best in their schools. Only a very small percentage of those who excel in college sports will be good enough to become professionals.

The same formula can be applied to a young musician of superior talent. The finest violinist or clarinetist in the entire high school system of a city may not be good enough to get into the best conservatories. You've got to be quite accomplished to even get a hearing from a topnotch school like Juilliard. There are other schools that offer fine music programs. But if you consider that there are only about 3,000 musicians who make a full-time living with symphony orchestras, you begin to see how competitive the field really is. The openings for serious singers and composers are even more restricted.

There are many fine classical musicians in America today who are not members of major symphony orchestras. These men and women still earn a good living by playing in smaller orchestras and supplementing their incomes by teaching. There are also musicians who leave symphony

FACT SHEET
PERFORMING AND COMPOSING CAREERS IN CLASSICAL
MUSIC

Career	Opportunities for Employment	Education and Training	Skills and Personality Traits
INSTRU-MENTAL-IST	1• Major Symphony Orchestras 2• Regional Symphony Orchestras 3• Metropolitan Orchestras 4• Ballets and Concerts, etc.	• Thorough knowledge of music • Intensive training through private study • Degree from conservatory or college with a strong music curriculum	• Musical talent • Versatility • Creative ability • Poise • Stage presence • Physical stamina
CONDUC-TOR (Musical Director)	• Same as Instrumentalist	• Same as instrumentalist with as much practical experience in playing and conducting as one can obtain	• Exceptional musical talent • Coordination • Ability to deal with people
SINGER	1• Recital Singer 2• Opera Chorus 3• Opera Soloist	• Broad background in music history and theory • Knowledge of foreign languages • Extensive training of voice through private study • Conservatory training desirable	• Same as instrumentalist plus: • Acting ability • Mastery of foreign languages • Sight singing • Ability to memorize quickly

Lifestyle	Earnings	Employment Outlook
• Night and week-end work • Considerable time spent in practice and rehearsal • Long and irregular hours • Performances often require travel • Hard to obtain year-round work	1• Average salary for a 40–54 week season—$30,000 2• $90–$270 per week (minimum salary 3• Approx. $25–$50 per concert 4• Approx. $25–$100 per concert	• The number of qualified applicants is increasing faster than the number of openings • Competition less keen in small communities
• Similar to instrumentalist Musical director must become involved with all aspects of putting on a concert season	• Earnings on every level slightly above those of a top-paid musician • Six figure income at highest levels	• Very limited
• Night and week-end work • Seasonal • Difficulty in obtaining regular employment • Singing career relatively short	1• Min. $200 per performance 2• Approx. $400 per week 3• $200–$4,000 per performance	• Competition keen • Very few opportunities to make a full-time living singing opera

FACT SHEET
PERFORMING AND COMPOSING CAREERS IN CLASSICAL
MUSIC

Career	Opportunities for Employment	Education and Training	Skills and Personality Traits
COMPOSER	• Extremely limited • A few composer-in-residence positions available in universities • Grants from foundations or government arts organizations	• Degree from conservatory desirable • Most professionals advise training in some related field—such as music education—to provide secure income	• Knowledge of scoring for all musical instruments • Ability to communicate one's ideas on paper • Thorough understanding of music theory and the styles one is working with • Self-discipline • Public relations skills to get people to listen to one's work
ARTIST IN RESIDENCE	• Colleges and Universities	• Same as instrumentalist • Academic credentials somewhat more important	• Same as instrumentalist plus: • Teaching abilities

orchestras because they can not take the extensive traveling involved. These fine musicians often become artists in residence at major universities. These positions entail performing as well as teaching.

Most people who become successful performers in the

Lifestyle	Earnings	Employment Outlook
• No regular hours • Serious composers must look elsewhere for job security	• Expect to make no money unless you are willing to write music that is commercial or "functional"—such as background music for T.V. or films	• More limited here than in any other field
• Balanced program of rehearsal, performance, and teaching advanced students • Less demanding work and more creative freedom than musicians in symphony orchestras	• Same pay scale as other college faculty (Approx. $13,000–$42,000)	• Opportunities are extremely scarce • Not likely to improve

classical field are aware of an exceptional talent by their early teens, although singers often blossom at a later age. Many of our finest instrumentalists are accomplished players by their sixth or seventh birthdays. Singers tend to develop later because their voices are still changing through-

Violinist Dmitry Sitkovetsky. (EUGENE NETZER)

out their teens. But any person who plans to make a career in classical performing will have to devote years of study and commitment before he or she can even begin to get an idea of how far they can go.

Finding the Right Teacher

Most performers and educators agree that it is vitally important for a young, talented person to connect with the right teacher as soon as possible. This can be accomplished in small towns as well as big cities. There are many fine teachers scattered throughout America, as well as financial aid programs for talented young people from poorer families. Great care must be taken in searching out the best teachers. Otherwise, the most gifted young musician may not reach his or her full potential.

Peter Mennin, president of the Juilliard School, suggests that young musicians and their parents spend some time researching the best teachers in their area.

There are a great number of wonderful private teachers throughout the country. But you can't take anyone's word about who they are. You have to find someone who knows what will be expected later, when the student will face the stiff competition of a place like Juilliard. You can get a list of accredited music schools from the *National Association of Schools of Music* in Reston, Virginia . . . but there are no real ratings or fast formulas.

The best teacher for one person isn't always good for someone else. The chemistry between teacher and student is very important. We get talented people from the most obvious, and also the most unlikely, places throughout the country. We're aware of many of the very best teachers. But sometimes people get excellent backgrounds from teachers we never heard of.

Conductor Gerard Schwarz believes that a person living in even the most remote areas can find a qualified teacher within driving distance. He is quick to point out that even as a high school student living in a nearby suburb of New York, he had to travel an hour and a half to take lessons.

> I had to take four buses and a train to get to my teacher's house, but I wanted those lessons. If you want it enough, there are fine instrumentalists all over the country who don't want to play in orchestras. They'd rather teach in universities. There are also many small orchestras and they all have some qualified musicians in them.

Now with piano or voice, it may be more difficult. But on most instruments, it's not too difficult to find a good teacher if you really go after it. But again, it's mostly up to the individual. Ask yourself, do I really want it bad enough? And remember, nobody's going to hand it to you on a silver platter.

Getting into a Music Conservatory

Conservatories are essentially colleges that specialize in music and other performing arts such as dance and theatre. People who apply for admission to one of the better conservatories have usually studied with a respected private teacher for many years and have reason to believe that they are people with exceptional talent. Anyone who is uncertain about his or her talent would probably be better off majoring in music at a liberal arts college where a broader educational background can be obtained.

Before a young musician is invited to audition for a major conservatory like Juilliard, his or her application is carefully screened by a faculty committee. Peter Mennin lists the basic qualities that the Juilliard School considers in its screening process. Other major conservatories generally follow similar guidelines.

> People are screened out if they don't have the right repertoire or if they haven't studied the composers that we want them to know. Each student must also submit a number of let-

ters of recommendation. After the initial screening, there might be twenty-five people competing for each opening. So our job is to pick the ones that will have the best chance of making a major career. . . .

We are looking for people of unquestioned talent. We may not accept a person with very good training who doesn't have much talent. We'll sometimes take a person who is a diamond in the rough, but with the potential to become a major talent. We try to look at what is going to happen to a person ten years from now. Does he or she have the kind of talent that deserves all the effort we are going to bring to bear, or is he or she just another talented person who wants to become well-rounded?

When a person applies for admission, he or she must list all the works that he is prepared to play for a jury and submit recommendations from his teacher. But you really can't judge a person until you hear him. Some kids haven't had the advantage of studying some of the music we expect them to know. We sometimes overlook that, especially with younger applicants.

If a person fails his or her audition, no reason is given unless the student or the teacher insists on it. Peter Mennin admits that the judges can only select those people who audition well. He points to specific things that are considered while the applicant is playing: "Is the person talented enough? Does he or she have enough demonstrated technique? Does the applicant sound like someone with a good chance of building a major career?"

Tuition

The cost of receiving a higher education is constantly rising. Whereas parents were once able to send their children to college as a matter of course, they now think twice before investing tens of thousands of dollars on a person who is not really motivated. Anyone applying to a place like

Juilliard is probably a dedicated and serious individual. But what happens to a talented young musician who just does not have the money to see his way through?

"I never want a student not to get into Juilliard because of a lack of money," says Peter Mennin. "If somebody is poor, we will give him a full scholarship. Seventy-five percent of our students get some kind of assistance. There are many talented people here who have no money at all, but they are still here. We get no government help. So it is part of the school's job to raise money from private sources."

The Audition

Let's assume that a person has the talent, gets to a top conservatory, and is now musically prepared to go out and compete in this crowded and difficult field. This individual will have to develop another crucial skill—the ability to audition well. In recent years, symphony orchestras have made it a point to eliminate discrimination and favoritism in selecting new members. The orchestra first advertises the vacancy in *International Musician*, a publication of the American Federation of Musicians. All applications are invited. Those players who seem to have an adequate background and knowledge of certain orchestral repertoire are invited to audition.

Although an orchestra's music director generally makes the final decision, the hiring responsibilities are most often shared by a committee. Musicians perform behind a black cloth screen so that the judges can only go by the sounds they hear. This method eliminates any personal preference or selections based on race or sex discrimination. In addition, the judges are usually scattered around the hall so that they can not discuss the performances among themselves.

On the surface, this method of auditioning seems fair. But there are a number of factors which do not necessarily favor the best musician landing the job. Auditions are pressure-filled situations that favor the person who can keep cool under the gun. Career coach Adele Scheele points out that in spite of all the attempts at making these auditions fair, there are no truly fair routes to success.

"Suppose one is poor at auditioning but great in the longer run?" she asks. "And, of course, there are also people who audition very well but don't really pull through in the long run. But that's life. Somehow a person must learn to audition so that his abilities can be appreciated."

There are also some heavy financial demands involved in auditioning for major symphony orchestras. "The conservatories are turning out far too many people for too few jobs," says Michael Wilcok, manager of the Houston Philharmonic. "Whenever we have a vacancy, we have many people show up for auditions. Most of those people are going to be turned down.

"A musician applying for a position these days must be prepared to spend a substantial amount of money. Every time a person comes to Houston for an audition, she must pay her own transportation and lodging. This can easily run into a thousand dollars or more. And remember, they have to do the same thing every time they go to another city to audition."

For obvious reasons, symphony orchestras tend to favor more experienced musicians. Players' applications are often rejected on the basis of previous musical background. There have been a number of cases of young musicians being turned down on the basis of experience who auditioned under another name and got the position. There has even been some discussion of eliminating auditions and bringing people up through a kind of minor league orchestra system, something like the one baseball uses. There are, in fact, a number of fine training orchestras, such as the one sponsored by the National Orchestral Association in New

York. But for the most part, auditions are a way of life. If you plan to make your living as a performer in the classical music field, you had better do more than learn how to play your instrument. Because if you do not learn how to audition well, you are probably not going to make it.

Lifestyle and Money

As orchestra manager of the New York Philharmonic, Henry Fogel has a unique perspective on the lifestyle of a classical musician. When the musicians' union negotiates for more money and benefits for its members, Fogel is a part of the management team that tries to minimize the commitment of the orchestra members. Yet he is well aware of the physical and emotional strain that musicians experience.

> The pressure of performing has never been fully studied. . . . How can you negotiate away the pressures of having to play the right notes at exactly the right split second? The pressures are the greatest when we go on tour. We always take a doctor with us. As a manager, I am always aware of the tremendous pressures under which performers operate . . . especially on tours. My job is to remove any external factor that adds to the tension so that it doesn't become unbearable. Remember, these musicians are away from their homes and families, eating strange food, dealing with a foreign language which they may not understand, dealing with different acoustics, sitting in a different position on an unfamiliar stage, and playing for an unfamiliar audience. As managers, we try to make sure that they have no other problems.

The New York Philharmonic, like most major orchestras, has a forty-week season. During these weeks, the musician is required to work approximately thirty hours. But Henry Fogel points out that the time commitment is actually much greater.

Two or three days a week, the musicians have to come in at 10 A.M. for a three-hour rehearsal and then come back for a concert at 8 P.M. That means that the time spent commuting is considerable. Also, most musicians practice several hours a day, and that too must be considered as a part of the job.

The salary for a musician in the New York Philharmonic is around $30,000 a year (plus a good benefits package). They also get paid for extra rehearsals and extra concerts. Many of the players teach, play in chamber groups and on recording sessions. Maybe Leonard Bernstein, Zubin Mehta, and a few others make a large income. But most orchestral musicians don't make a great deal of money, although one can do reasonably well.

CONDUCTING

In the past, it was the great instrumental soloists who were the stars of the classical music world. But the emergence of talented, charismatic personalities like Bernstein and Mehta have placed conductors in the forefront of public attention. Aside from being a highly acclaimed conductor, Gerard Schwarz has made his mark as a musician and teacher. His insights into the world of serious music cover a wide range of issues and present an informative picture for those seeking careers in this field.

Gerard Schwarz reflects on his life as a musician and conductor

At the age of thirty-five, Gerard Schwarz has gained a reputation as one of the most well-respected young conductors in America. After spending four years as the co-principal trumpet player with the New York Philharmonic, he turned his full attention to conducting. He is currently the Music Director of the Y Chamber Symphony in New York, the Los Angeles Chamber Orchestra, the Waterloo

Zubin Mehta conducts a rehearsal of the New York Philharmonic. (MARIANNE BARCELLONA)

Village Festival in New Jersey, and the White Mountains Festival in New Hampshire. He has also appeared as guest conductor for the American Symphony, the Detroit Symphony, the San Francisco Symphony, and the Jerusalem Symphony.

It is not unusual for a conductor to be an accomplished instrumentalist. In fact, most good conductors think of themselves as musicians first.

This makes sense. For if a conductor is to get the most out of an orchestra, he or she must be aware of the discipline involved in mastering an instrument. "It is that kind of discipline," Gerard Schwarz notes, "that is more important than almost anything else. One needs the discipline to see something through. To understand the difficulties and then master them."

BECOMING A CLASSICAL MUSICIAN

Most aspiring classical musicians will not be able to find full-time positions in major symphony orchestras. It takes years to find out just how high a level one is capable of achieving. Gerard Schwarz firmly believes that dedication and commitment are the most important elements from the beginning.

If you decide that you want to be a musician, then you study as hard as you can. You work at it and you practice like crazy. You only know after all the studying is done whether you really have a chance. Of course, if you're not coordinated enough to play the instrument, or if you have no rhythmic sense, then you're not going to get anywhere. But if you decide that music is what you really care about in your life, you can get pretty far as a student on interest and dedication alone.

The decision to become a professional is another matter completely. There has to be a tremendous amount of talent there to have any chance at all. Sometimes a talent blossoms early, and sometimes you can't even tell at age twenty.

By the time he was accepted at New York's High School of Performing Arts, Gerard Schwarz felt that he had exceptional talent for music. On the other hand, his was not a case of the child prodigy who was an accomplished musician at age seven or eight.

My parents were from Vienna, and everyone in the family was given piano lessons from the time we were five. We lived in New Jersey and often went to the ballet and opera in New York. When I was seven, I saw a performance of the opera *Aida*. I decided that I wanted to play the trumpet because I loved the marvelous grand march. My parents weren't too thrilled about their son being a trumpet player, although they didn't exactly discourage me.

When I was in the third grade, I went to the music teacher and told him that I wanted to play the trumpet. He said I would have to wait until fourth grade. The next year I came back. He asked me to toot on a mouthpiece and told me that I would do fine. I did very well with the trumpet. Within a few weeks, I was picking out tunes. Of course, I knew how to read music from my piano training and that was a great help.

When I was twelve, I tried out for the National Music Camp at Interlochen, Michigan. I was very nervous about getting in because I didn't think I was very good. I became the first trumpet player that summer, although they said that it was the worst trumpet section they ever had. By the time I went back the next summer, I decided that I wanted to be a professional musician. . . . By the third summer, I was really pursuing it, and my parents allowed me to attend the High School of Performing Arts the following year. But those summers at Interlochen really did it for me.

By the time he started high school, Gerry was accepted into New York's All City Orchestra. He also sought out as many opportunities to play as he could find.

I played in a different orchestra every night. I also studied and practiced as hard as I could.

After I graduated Performing Arts, I was accepted at Juilliard. I also auditioned for the American Brass Quintet. That was a big deal for me because I had been recommended by my former trumpet teacher. At first, I was turned down because they were afraid that I would be drafted into the Army. But six months later, they were stuck, so they took me. I had done a number of professional jobs from the time I was sixteen. But that was the beginning of an important part of my professional career. After that, I played in a chamber music group for eight years. Then I joined the American Symphony and did a lot of other work as well. At the same time, I was still completing my studies at Juilliard.

GOING FROM MUSICIAN TO CONDUCTOR

Gerard Schwarz began his conducting career at the age of seventeen. He spent four years developing his career by leading the orchestra for the Eric Hawkins Dance Company. He also conducted a small group called the Soho Ensemble. Samuel Lipman, the noted pianist, was one of the first to encourage Gerard to devote his life to conducting.

"Another conductor got sick a week before a performance of Elliot Carter's piano concerto, and I was asked to fill in," Gerard continues. "Samuel Lipman was impressed with my work. He pushed very hard for me to become a conductor. But at that time, I was more interested in becoming a great trumpet player."

After he joined the New York Philharmonic, Gerard resumed his career as a part-time conductor. Eventually, he decided that he wanted to devote all of his energies to conducting. He felt that it would be impossible to continue playing with the orchestra at the same time.

Conductor Gerard Schwarz prepares for a concert. (THOMAS VICTOR)

As extraordinary an experience as playing in the New York Philharmonic is, it's just not the same as having touch with the whole work of art, the whole orchestra, the whole programming. And that's what I wanted as a human being. I wanted to get involved with the music on as high a level as possible.

Gerard Schwarz describes conducting as a combination of musical talent, coordination, an understanding of people, and the ability to lead. These are the tools he believes all good conductors must possess:

> To start with, you must have a *good ear.* You have to be coordinated so that you can communicate with your hands what you want the orchestra to do. You have to be smart enough to deal with musicians as your colleagues. And at the same time, you must have their respect. After all, you are telling them what to do.
>
> Talent for conducting isn't always as easy to judge as instrumental talent. If a pianist misses a note, it's very clear to everyone. So in a way, it's easier to evaluate their performance. . . . But the main thing for anyone who wants to become a conductor is to devote your time to studying music and watch different conductors.
>
> When I was with the New York Philharmonic, I studied every conductor that came in, seeing what they did right or wrong. I watched how they got musicians to play well, or how they sometimes offended members of the orchestra. I tried to get a feeling for each conductor's ideas. And I also learned a great deal about how a complex organization like the New York Philharmonic is run.

MUSICAL DIRECTORS AND GUEST CONDUCTORS

The most successful conductors often become musical directors of the orchestras they conduct. This position requires an involvement with every phase of running the orchestra. The music director must deal with administrative and business matters in conjunction with the orchestra's board of directors. Aside from all the responsibilities of conducting, the music director must plan an entire musical season—from selecting musical pieces to deciding which soloists and guest conductors will be used.

"A music director is someone who has the ability to assume all the duties of conducting," Gerard Schwarz remarks. "He must also have an organized mind so that he can lead an orchestra administratively as well as musically. If something's not right, the music director is usually held responsible no matter what the problem might be."

Most orchestras like to employ guest conductors at various points in a season. This gives the musicians and audiences an opportunity to have the musical selections interpreted in different ways. This sytem also allows conductors to work with a number of orchestras. Gerard Schwarz points out that guest conducting has its advantages as well as its drawbacks:

> When you are a guest conductor, you don't have to do a lot of the work—like hiring players and dealing with other personnel problems. All I have to do as a guest conductor is to prepare my program. But there are other problems. If I'm the musical director of an orchestra, those musicians know my ideas. . . . They know my concept of sound and they're familiar with the language that I use. So we begin at a very high level.
>
> But when you are a guest conductor, you have to decide if you are going to try to make the orchestra and the music sound your way. I will sometimes try to seat the musicians the way I seat my orchestras, which is a different configuration than what other conductors use. I may try to get them to use my concept of string sound. But sometimes, strong players resist. And I don't blame them for resisting.
>
> If my orchestra in Los Angeles plays a certain way for me, that's how they'll play for anyone, because that's how they've been trained. If a guest conductor comes in with a sound that's different than mine, they will automatically resist. . . . So you

first have to see where an orchestra is and then go with the flow. You must pick and choose just where and how you will change things. In my early years of guest conducting, I would just say: "Okay, this is what I believe and bam!" But I quickly realized that this wasn't always the best way.

In principle, guest conductors should not make as great concerts as the main conductor of an orchestra. But on occasion, a guest conductor will give an outstanding concert.

PURSUING A CAREER AS A CONDUCTOR

Any young person who is serious about conducting as a career should attempt to master at least one orchestral instrument aside from the piano. It is not absolutely necessary to first become a musician in a major symphony orchestra, although such an experience would be most helpful.

"Observe as many conductors as you can," Gerard Schwarz advises.

Often a person can get permission to watch. Or one can say to a conductor: "I want to be a conductor." Then you offer to put yourself at his disposal. Say to him: "Look, I'll mark your parts. I'll do bowings. I'll do research for you." You also learn a great deal by playing in an orchestra. Then you just have to get your craft down by going out and doing it.

Put together some kind of small group that you can conduct. After you get some experience, try to get to a good conservatory like Juilliard or audition for the American Symphony Orchestra League.

The two most important things I did in training for conducting was playing in a chamber music group and then joining the New York Philharmonic. The chamber music group helped me learn to work with my colleagues and use time effectively. . . . Now I do forty concerts a year in Los Angeles and twenty-five in New York. That would be enough . . . but in this field one's life is almost endless, I also guest conduct

Victoria Bond—the first woman to receive a Ph.D. in conducting from Juilliard. (COURTESY OF AFFILIATE ARTISTS)

with a number of major orchestras both here and abroad. It's really a very exciting life, and it can come about through a combination of talent, good opportunities, and knowing what you're doing. All of that. Plus luck.

118

Victoria Bond Speaks About Assistant Conductors and Women in Classical Music

The principal conductor of every major orchestra has an assistant. In the course of the long season, the assistant conductor will conduct a number of subscription and student concerts. If the main conductor of an orchestra becomes sick or is called out of town, the assistant conductor will take over.

Like most assistant conductors in similar positions, Victoria Bond had extensive conducting experience before she was appointed assistant conductor to Andre Previn at the Pittsburgh Symphony Orchestra. She has been featured as a guest conductor with a number of chamber groups and smaller orchestras like the New Amsterdam Symphony Orchestra in New York. But unlike most of the important conductors of the past and present, Victoria Bond is a woman.

It is no secret that women have not been given many opportunities as conductors of serious music. Traditionally, the few women conductors were involved with vocal music. "Women in orchestras is a recent phenomenon," Ms. Bond explains. "Major orchestras all over the world still don't have women conductors."

Because she is an attractive and petite woman, people always ask her if musicians have a problem taking direction from her. "On a social level, people won't take you seriously if you're a petite woman," Ms. Bond states candidly. "But once you are up on the podium, professional musicians will respond to your vibes as a conductor. Other things don't matter. . . . But women in orchestras are still very rare."

Victoria Bond's chances of eventually becoming music director of a major orchestra are probably as good as any young woman conductor in America today. In her role as assistant to a major personality like Andre Previn, she is constantly being watched and evaluated by managers of other orchestras. She is well aware of the tools she will need to succeed as a music director.

> The job involves a lot more than conducting. It involves dealing with the business of running a symphony orchestra: Planning a whole season, knowing how to put soloists together, dealing with a board of directors. Its scope goes into economics, sociology, and all sorts of other areas. There has never been a comprehensive (educational) program covering everything involved in the management and directorship of a symphony orchestra.

WORKING WITH MUSICIANS

Like Gerard Schwarz, Ms. Bond is very much aware of how important dealing with other people is for a successful conductor. This can sometimes be a difficult matter, particularly in large orchestras.

"It's not a question of brow-beating people. It's a question of working with people," Victoria Bond observes. "There are some conductors who can work with musicians effectively by projecting their enthusiasm and love of music making."

Anyone who has seen Gerard Schwarz conduct would agree that he is the kind of person Ms. Bond is talking about. But he has found that an open and cooperative approach to music making is not always so easy to accomplish. One would expect the members of a professional symphony orchestra to be mature and disciplined people. But if a conductor does not gain their respect early in the game, a rehearsal hall can seem very much like a noisy third grade class with the teacher out of the room.

"Some of the older conductors were known for being tough . . . and in some ways ruthless," Gerard Schwarz recalls. "I'm beginning to understand how that can come about from all the pressures a conductor is under. . . . I remember once a very famous conductor was rehearsing the New York Philharmonic. The musicians weren't behaving because this conductor wasn't gaining their respect or attention. He said: 'Come on, guys! If you all get quiet, I'll let you out early for lunch.' I said to myself: 'What is this, kindergarten? Just do your job.' "

From all reports, there are members of many top symphony orchestras who are not as happy as one might expect. For one thing, serious music is a field where one is always striving for more. We have seen how difficult it is to become a member of a major symphony orchestra. Once a person gets there though, he or she may not be content to play third violin. A third violinist wants to play first violin, and a principal player may feel that he should be the featured soloist or music director. Although we can easily understand people feeling this way in a society that puts such a great emphasis on being *number one*, we would hope that a player in a great orchestra would feel a measure of satisfaction. Unfortunately, this is often not the case.

"Many orchestral musicians are frustrated people," Gerard Schwarz points out. "Friends of mine in other fields think that playing music for a living is an honor and a privilege. . . . It used to be that to play in the Vienna or Berlin Philharmonic wasn't frustrating. It was an honor to be a part of those great orchestras and not doing something else. That's been lost a little bit now."

ARTIST IN RESIDENCE

Violinist Sung Rai Sohn is one of a growing number of talented musicians who has little or no desire to be in an orchestra. As a student at Baltimore's Peabody Conservatory, Sung Rai got a taste of being an orchestral musician as an often-called substitute in the Baltimore Symphony Orchestra. Like Gerard Schwarz, he did not like the attitude of many orchestra members. He also had little desire to have his playing submerged in a twenty-person violin section.

> I always wanted to be a soloist. I felt that if that didn't work out, I would join an orchestra as a second choice. . . . I found that in many orchestras, some people didn't really care about what they were doing, and that turned me off. It seemed to me that many orchestral musicians see it as just a way to make money.

As an artist in residence at New York's Sarah Lawrence College, Sung Rai is part of the Lawrentian String Quartet.

> We choose all of our own music. We are the owners of our organization and we make all of the decisions. That's why I love it. After you have that, it's tough to go back to being an orchestra player. As an artist in residence, you have time for rehearsing, practicing, and giving master classes. We give one day to teaching and five days to rehearsing and performing. We rehearse from ten to five almost every day and perform very often.

As you might expect, it is extremely difficult to find artist in residence positions. This career allows the musician to have the security of being a part of a college faculty, the freedom to select the music he or she plays, and the exposure of a soloist. The traveling involved is much less extensive than with an orchestra. Since the college or university benefits greatly by maintaining a well-respected group of artists in residence, they permit the musicians a great deal of flexibility in working out their performing and teaching schedules. Under such ideal conditions, very few people are likely to surrender their positions.

"The opportunities for artists in residence are very

The Lawrentian String Quartet at Sarah Lawrence College (Sung Rai Sohn, seated).

scarce," says Sung Rai. "It is much easier to get into an orchestra, even though there can be eighty or ninety people competing for every opening. But at least the openings are announced in *International Musician*. It is often very difficult to find out where the openings for artists in residence are."

In spite of the competition and the tough job market, Sung Rai encourages talented young musicians to "take chances and see what develops." The majority of those who try will not make it. But those who do are among the lucky few who get the opportunity of making a living at something they really love.

CLASSICAL SINGER

The aspiring classical vocalist faces an even more difficult road than the young instrumentalist. First of all, there are far fewer opportunities. Only a few hundred individuals make a full-time income singing classical music. Furthermore, it is often difficult to spot an exceptional talent at an early age. Male voices sometimes do not fill out until a person is in his early twenties. A number of great female singers did not attain their full vocal range until they were well along in their studies. A person starting out must hope that her God-given pair of vocal chords develops in the right way. Bass-baritone Simon Estes recalls that he was still a high tenor during his senior year in high school. Soprano Birgit Nilsson was known as the soprano with no top at the beginning of her career.

Developing the Tools

Generally, classical singers must practice for years to develop the basic musical knowledge they will need to carry them through their careers. In addition, a young singer must develop correct vocal technique as soon as possible.

While instrumentalists can often get their bad habits corrected at a later stage in their education, a singer with bad habits can ruin his or her voice in a relatively short time. On the other hand, a sound technique can provide a singer with an extremely long career. Singers nurture their technique by pacing not only how much they sing, but the kinds of roles they sing.

Most successful classical singers make their marks singing opera. This requires the study of acting and body movement as well as the mastery of several foreign languages. Opera singer/educator Rise Stevens compares the work and training of an opera singer to that of an Olympic decathlon champion like Bruce Jenner. "Here was a superb athlete who had to train for years to excel in all facets of sports. The classical music vocalist is in much the same category. Except that in addition to physical training, he or she must master a musical and mental discipline that is in every way as rigorous as the physical one."

Breaking into the Field

There are numerous awards, grants, and competitions that are available to talented young singers. Information about these can be obtained by writing to the Central Opera Service at Lincoln Center for the Performing Arts, 1865 Broadway, New York, New York 10023. There has also been an increase in the number of smaller regional opera houses in this country as well as university workshops. Still, the number of opportunities for beginning opera singers in this country is extremely limited. Rise Stevens believes that a young, talented opera singer can do well by beginning his or her career in Europe.

> When I finished school and had several student opera productions to my credit, I was offered a contract at the Metropolitan (Opera Company in New York). Some instinct, however,

told me that I did not want to gain my experience and learn my parts in front of the (demanding) New York public and critics. I wanted to arrive as a finished artist. And so I decided to go to Europe. I joined the opera in Prague, Czechoslovakia, and had two years of the invaluable repertory training and experience that (is still) not available in this country. Then I felt that I was ready for the Met. I realize that many distinguished colleagues did not go that route. But I cannot help but think that their paths might have been easier if they had that work in back of them.

Financial Considerations

Like so many other performing arts careers, there is not much of a middle ground for a classical vocalist. The salary range for an opera singer is about $200 per performance for a small part in a regional opera company to $4,000 for a leading role at the Met. A recognized superstar like tenor Luciano Pavarotti can command even larger sums. On the other hand, there are many talented singers who must hold down other jobs in order to make ends meet.

Simon Estes on Overcoming Obstacles and Prejudice

If you decide on opera singing as your profession, you have chosen one of the most competitive of all performing careers. If you happen to be a black man, the odds of breaking through as an internationally recognized opera star are almost impossible. Simon Estes is one of the very few to overcome these odds. Now in his forties and regarded as one of the finest bass-baritone singers in the world, Simon has still not (as of this writing) been invited to sing opera at many of America's top opera houses. Though he is not a bitter man in any sense, Simon Estes makes no bones about the racial prejudice he has encountered throughout his career.

Bass-baritone Simon Estes performs in the opera "Die Walkure."

I hope the day will come where we don't have to talk about a color problem, but we can talk about the art and love of the art. . . . There were times during the sixties that I was very hurt by this racial thing because I could not break the (color) barrier to sing opera. I have no hatred or bitterness. But I do have a great deal of disappointment and sadness. Not for myself. But for the whole country—white people as well as blacks.

After years of acclaim in Europe's greatest opera houses, Simon Estes finally made his debut at America's most prestigious showplace—the Metropolitan Opera—on January 4, 1982. Although the role of the Landgrave in Wagner's "Tannhauser" is not the one Estes would have preferred for his Met debut, he decided to accept the part in order to encourage other talented black opera singers:

There are so many black singers out there that should be singing. But if they don't see anybody on the stage with whom to identify, they feel there's a void. . . . I have spoken at many schools, and black students often come up to me and say: "Why should I struggle? You should have sung at places like the New York Metropolitan Opera years ago . . . I feel the situation is hopeless." And I tell them: "Look, you've got to stay there and fight. You can make it. Yes, you're going to have to be head and shoulders above anybody else or you're not going to get the job. You're going to have to be almost perfect in every aspect because they don't leave room for any error for us. . . .

I feel that the administrators are at fault for this situation, not the audiences. . . . I've been able to sing all over the world. But I feel that it's a tragedy that I haven't been able to share my gift for the last seven or eight years at the Met. In Europe, the leaders of the major opera houses have told me that they can't understand why I'm not used more in my own country. And one of the top opera house administrators in Europe recently told me that he was positive that the reason must be because I am a Negro.

Simon Estes can trace elements of discrimination back to his freshman year at the University of Iowa where he was rejected from the school chorus. He has managed to hang in there and beat the odds. "The head of the University chorus said that my voice wasn't good enough and that I should probably try to sing some kind of popular music. But Charles Kellis—a voice teacher at the university—told me that I had the voice to sing opera. I didn't even know what opera was. But Mr. Kellis had confidence in me. He worked with me for five hours a day. The following year he suggested that I audition for Juilliard. He arranged an audition and I received a full scholarship."

Simon Estes on Learning Operatic Roles

Learning operatic parts is one of the most challenging tasks in musical performing. Many great opera stars come from operatic families and become familiar with operatic repertoire at a young age. Simon Estes did some singing in church as a youngster. But before he came to Juilliard, he was not particularly familiar with operatic roles. Remember that the mastery of an opera requires both the memorization of music, body movements, and words that are most often in a foreign language.

The first thing I do is get together with a vocal coach and start learning the music. Simultaneously, I will get a book and start reading about the story of that opera. Some singers like to learn the music first, then the story. Others like to learn the story before the music. But whenever possible, I like to do both at the same time. I find that it's easier to have a concept of the story while I am progressing with the music . . . I'm extremely busy and I don't have much time to learn new roles. Sometimes I have to learn a new role in a week or two. So I will study two or three hours a day with a coach, then I will go home and study the part privately, without singing.

I also listen to recordings, although some artists don't feel that you should listen to recordings. It's not that you imitate. But if you are pressed for time, as we all are in this fast-paced society of ours, it's very helpful to get the orchestration of an opera in your ear. And that also helps to save your voice because those two little vocal chords only have so many miles in them. So I try to get as many recordings of an opera as possible. I like to hear the way each conductor and each singer does it.

I will sometimes spend eight or nine hours a day learning a new role. If I'm really cramped for time, I will wake up in the middle of the night to memorize an opera. Because of the time situation and the pressure that I'm under, I'm very grateful that I can memorize a new role in five or six days if I have to.

The Solo Recital

Many classical vocalists begin their careers singing solo recitals with the accompaniment of only a piano. These recitals can be staged in smaller halls at a far lower cost than any opera. Because of the difficulty that black males experience when they try to break into opera, Simon Estes did more recital singing at the beginning of his career than most other performers of his caliber. He feels that if vocalists would spend more time singing recitals at the beginning of their careers, their voices would last longer and they would be better musicians.

The recital is the most difficult kind of singing. You need more purity and clarity of sound because you are totally exposed. There is only one instrument, the piano, and you. When you sing a recital you have much more direct contact with an audience and you must communicate differently than you would in an opera. Recital singing is more difficult; there is more pressure. Generally, you do more singing in a recital than you do in an opera. . . . You sometimes have to sing for an hour and a half. This helps you build up stamina and durability.

Learning Foreign Languages

Although there is a trend in America toward performing operas in English, most classical singers have to master their operatic roles in the original language. Vocalists agree that the operas of Richard Wagner are among the most difficult to master. The challenge is far greater when these roles are sung in the original German in front of a demanding German audience. Can you imagine the pressures Simon Estes experienced as the first black man to sing at the famed Bayreuth Festival in Germany?

> I must admit that I was nervous because Bayreuth is the pinnacle of Wagnerian music and all the Wagnerian fanatics come there. . . . Because I was the first black man to sing there, the newspapers said that they were expecting some demonstrations and rioting. There were no problems, but it was an unusual amount of pressure. I had a tremendous amount of success and I've been invited back to the Festival every year. Most of the German critics agreed that I sang my part better than any of the German singers.
>
> Before I started singing opera, I never realized that I had a talent for langauges. I had taken Latin in college because I originally planned to be a doctor. I learned to speak German pretty well and then I learned to speak Italian. I also can speak some Russian and Spanish. I can't speak French but I can sing in French. In Europe, listeners are very concerned with pronunciation and diction. And I have found that this need to have good diction in foreign languages also helps in one's native tongue.

CLASSICAL COMPOSERS

"There is nobody I know of in America making their complete living as a composer doing nothing but symphonic work," says Morton Gould, one of America's most successful classical composers. "The only way to work full-time at classical composing is to be born into wealth or to marry a wealthy person. That's the only way one has the luxury to spend the enormous amount of time it takes to put a serious piece of music together without worrying about paying the rent."

Morton Gould has made a good living by composing what he calls "functional music" for films, television, theatre, and ballet. His credits include the score for the television mini-series movie *Holocaust* and the Broadway show *Million Dollar Baby*. Because this kind of composing appeals to a much larger audience, a composer can collect an accumulated income from performing rights. Gould explains how he adapts his skills to the various mediums:

> No matter what you write music for, you try to write the best you possibly can within the confines of what that music is meant to be. . . . All different musical climates have their own value. You can write a bad symphony or a great pop tune. The key is to come up with something that is inventive, creative, and fresh sounding. . . . Obviously, a film score like *Holocaust* can't get into the kinds of complexities as a symphony I might write. . . .
>
> But basically, one cannot survive by just writing serious music. It's as simple as that. Anyone who wants to become a serious composer should make sure that they are equipped to do something else. That something else might be teaching, coaching, arranging, copying music, or a number of other things. If you can teach, then at least you have something that society needs. But if you're just sitting with compositions that you want performed, there's no urgency about that, except for yourself. So you must give yourself the strength and security of a means of economic support.

Becoming a Classical Composer

Any person who is interested in serious composing should get to a qualified teacher as soon as possible. In fact, many composition students go to a number of teachers in order to perfect different techniques. Here are some basic guidelines that Morton Gould suggests:

Composer Morton Gould conducting a studio orchestra recording one of his new compositions. (J. HABIG)

Listen to a great deal of music. Learn as much as you can. Be curious. Try to develop a strong critical sense for your own work. Everyone who writes feels that he is going to be the next Bach or Mozart, because composing is an act of ego. It may be cruel to say, but sometimes there's more ego than talent involved.

An aspiring composer should get to a place where he can hear his music. Get to a university where you can use the musicians as a workshop. This is like an apprenticeship for a composer. It's unlikely that a professional orchestra will try out a piece by an unproven person. Try to get your work to smaller groups or solo performers. Sometimes music for a particular instrument might be in great demand. For example, we've just come through a period where there has been a tremendous run on guitar and flute music. Also, you might get a publisher interested in some compositions for bands or school orchestras, and he might agree to accept some of your more serious stuff. Publishers are looking for new works by new composers. But it doesn't make sense for them to take only stuff that they can't sell.

Young people are always asking me how to get started. There are really no hard and fast rules. In some cases, I'll look at their music and tell them that they have talent. Other times, I'll try to tactfully tell them that what they are doing isn't going to work. It's very tough out there, but I believe that a real vital talent will show itself at one point or another.

Dealing with the Competition

A composer of classical music must be both patient and aggressive if he or she expects to make any headway. By comparison, there are many more opportunities for the gifted performer than for a talented composer. Conductors like Gerard Schwarz get hundreds of scores that they don't even ask for. "Eventually, I listen to everything," Schwarz promises. "But it can take months before I have time to get to it. Imagine how much time and postage are involved in just sending all this stuff back." Still, most conductors want to occasionally program music to help educate audiences and introduce new composers.

"Composers must be very aggressive and good con men," says Audrey Michaels, an experienced public relations person in the classical field. "Their publishers are often lax and don't work very hard for them. So the contemporary composer has to really get in there and pitch himself constantly . . . because the most persistent ones are the ones who get people to listen to them."

Morton Gould agrees that all composers must learn how to hustle. "But there are some dangers," he points out.

People will notice you if you're aggressive. But you can also turn them off if you're not careful. For example, it's a big mistake to come up to a conductor right after a performance and attempt to give him your tape. Conductors of major symphony orchestras are so deluged with scores and tapes that they hardly have time to catch up with the work they're supposed to be doing. Where are they going to find the time for every newcomer who just shows up?

Still, a composer must find a way to make his work known so that the right people become aware of it. In some cases, you can develop a contact who will say to a conductor: "Hey, I know a talented young composer. You really ought to take a look at his score." Older composers often become mentors and patrons of younger colleagues. But there are so few new pieces performed that the older composer might be hurting his own chances by pushing someone else's work. Still, there is a long history of more established composers encouraging and helping young ones. . . .

I will always try to find some time to talk to young people. But I have friends that just refuse to give that time. There are some very well-known figures who are accessible. And there are others who are totally inaccessible. They don't want anybody coming up and talking to them. Maybe they'll agree to see somebody if a dear friend asks them to do it as a favor. But they feel that it's an imposition on their time, because they are busy—still trying to fulfill themselves.

Outlook

There are always going to be some opportunities for new serious composers. But they are likely to be extremely limited. Morton Gould believes that the prospects are likely to get worse.

Many of the classical publishers have been taken over by big conglomerates, and there are fewer of them. There is very little of the old kind of personal attention that you could get from a number of different publishers. If one didn't like your music, you had a fighting chance with another. That's much more limited now.

There are many more new composers in this country who are quite good. But like everything else, classical music is tied up with economics. It's possible that orchestras will have less rehearsal time in the future, and it takes a lot of time to master a new piece. For the most part, the symphony orchestra audience wants to hear things that are familiar.

There are no kits or tools that can be handed out to anybody to insure success. It's tough out there. That's why a young composer should develop some practical skills—either in music or in another business. . . . The idea that a composer should have to work for a living at something other than music isn't a very comfortable idea. But it is a very real one.

The number of people who did only composing and nothing else for a living is very few—even going back to the classical period. Some composers were patronized by courts and princes. But if the prince's son had a birthday, Mozart or Haydn would have to write some kind of practical piece of music that would be understood by the people there.

"Compromising" Your Work

Morton Gould is not uncomfortable composing music that is more practical or functional in nature. He tries to write the best possible music he can, no matter what the assignment. But many other serious composers find that they lose their inspiration if they work in more popular forms like television and film soundtracks. In discussing his feelings about serious composing, Juilliard's president, Peter Mennin, makes a clear distinction between composing for the sake of art and composing as a job. Here are some of the things that Mennin—a highly regarded composer in his own right—feels aspiring composers should keep in mind:

If you can do without composing, then do without it. But some people have no choice. They must compose. Almost nobody makes a living being a "longhair" composer. If you want to go into rock or popular music, that's different. But for those of us who don't want to write, or even listen to rock, it's another story. Classical composing is a commitment. It's a way of life in which you have to find other ways to sustain yourself. There never has been that much of a market for the composer with serious musical ideas. First of all, it's very advanced music that's not very easy for most people to take. So unless someone has a deep commitment that this is what he wants to do with his life, forget it. And unless you have that commitment, you're not going to be very good anyhow. A serious composer writes from his gut. If you don't stick with it, you become just another journeyman trying to make a living.

If you do things like background music for films, you've got to give up any notions that you're creating art. At some point, a composer has to make a decision about what he is going to do. You can either treat it as a job at which you can do very well or you think about it as an art. Unfortunately, they don't mix as well as one could like.

BUSINESS CAREERS IN CLASSICAL MUSIC

Artist Management

"We're not in the kind of profession that's looking to exploit a six-month hit record," explains Sheldon Gold of ICM Artists. "We're looking to build a thirty, forty, or fifty-year career." This is the kind of attitude that a manager of classical performers must take. Unlike the popular music business, there are very few "flash in the pan" type performers connected with classical music.

People who become successful classical artists are products of tremendous innate talents and long years of study. But no performing artist—no matter how great—can reach his or her full potential without proper management. As the president of a company that represents such notables as violinists Itzhak Perlman, flutist James Galway, and ballet dancer Mikhail Baryshnikov, Sheldon Gold understands

FACT SHEET
BUSINESS CAREERS IN CLASSICAL MUSIC

Career	Opportunities for Employment	Education and Training	Skills and Personality Traits
ARTIST MANAGEMENT (Finding work for clients and developing their careers)	1• Representing only 1 or 2 artists 2• Specializing in only musicians, singers, or conductors 3• Working for a major agency	• College education helpful; courses in business, psychology, accounting and law • Some managers have law degrees or MBA's • A course or seminar in arts administration is usually recommended instead of a degree in arts administration • Internship or involvement in college committee that plans and implements concerts	• An understanding of business principles • A love of music • An appreciation of the artist's problems • Ability to deal with all kinds of people • Ability to work under pressure

the qualities that make successful managers as well as successful performers.

The manager's job is to make sure that the artists have the means to do what they are expected to do when they walk out on the stage. Nobody arrives with a label that says "artist manager." You evolve into that by learning every aspect of what this business requires. . . .

Sheldon Gold does hire new people from time to time. Here is what he looks for in an aspiring artist manager:

Lifestyle	Earnings	Employment Outlook
• Willingness to make your job the major part of your life • Little separation between work and social life • Long hours, nights, and weekends	• Highly variable, depending on the success of one's artists • Six-figure income possible on top rungs of the ladder	• Limited number of opportunities, but highly qualified people are in great demand

I need someone who is going to go out and book artists in local areas. Someone who is willing to travel all over the country and assist with the programming and travel arrangements. These representatives protect the artist from (ICM's) point of view by acting as a buffer between the artist and the general public. Some of our beginning people involve themselves with publicity and promotional work. They start out by fulfilling publicity requisitions and eventually they prepare their own written materials. So there are a number of ways to get involved. But there is no magic pill for success.

FACT SHEET
BUSINESS CAREERS IN CLASSICAL MUSIC

Career	Opportunities for Employment	Education and Training	Skills and Personality Traits
ORCHESTRA ADMINISTRATION (Management of all the business aspects pertaining to a symphony orchestra)	1• Executive director 2• Assistant manager 3• Director of development 4• Director of public relations 5• Controller 6• Director of ticket sales	• College background • Recommended involvement with college committee that plans the institution's concert season specializing in the area of one's particular interests • General business background with an eye toward an area of specialization • Credit bearing internship if possible	• Same as above plus: • Skills in negotiations with various unions • Community involvement • A general understanding of fund raising, marketing, and public relations techniques

Opportunities at a company like ICM Artists are limited. Although it is one of the biggest companies in its field. ICM only employs about twenty people. "I get many resumes," says Sheldon Gold. "But I usually give first priority to people in the organization. If I have a person here who is capable of moving up, I'd rather build from underneath. Two of our people came from the record business. Several came from other areas of the music business and began at a lower rung here than at their former jobs. One of our people in the program department was hired right out of college."

Lifestyle	Earnings	Employment Outlook
• Night and week-end work • Long hours	• Moderate to good income • Top orchestra administrators make low six figure salaries • Compensation for comparable work is greater in most other areas of business	• Good for ambitious and highly qualified people

Getting Started

"Unless you're caught up in the disease, don't even think about this field," advises Sheldon Gold. Artist management is a field that requires dedication and long hours. So ask yourself if you are willing to make your job your life, because that is what almost all successful managers must do. But if you do have classical music in your blood and you want to get involved, there are a number of steps you can take.

While you are in high school, you can broaden your

scope by learning about music and speaking to music business professionals. In college, you can get involved in planning and implementing concerts. Once you have some knowledge and experience under your belt, you can approach the field from a number of directions. Some managers only represent one or two artists. Some specialize in only conductors or singers. Other managers involve themselves only with making deals in foreign countries. So you must evaluate the possibilities and see which approach suits you best. Naturally, any part-time experience or internship you can line up while still in school would be most helpful.

Education and Training

There are no specific educational requirements for entering the field of artist management, although most managers do have a college background. A number of programs in arts management are currently being offered at various universities. One of the strongest critics of these programs is Harold Shaw, president of Shaw Artists.

I haven't seen one degree program in arts management that I really like. The educators designing these programs have no idea of what happens to the student once he graduates. It's rather sad that such programs are not designed by the professional people along with the educators, so that they are more geared to the real world outside of school. Instead, you're only getting an idea of what an educator thinks of arts management. And the chances are that educator has never been professionally involved in the field.

Not all professionals would agree with Shaw's harsh evaluation. But it certainly makes sense to seek out only those courses and degree programs that involve professional managers and administrators as part of the educational process. The American Symphony Orchestra League can provide a list of schools with arts administration programs. But you are the only one who can really ascertain just how useful they are. Remember, most colleges and universities are in business to make a profit. They tend to offer those programs and courses that will attract students. So you had better speak to the people who are involved with these programs before you spend your time and money.

Dealing with People

Managers are in the personal service business. They must know how to handle the personal problems of temperamental artists. At the same time, they must know how to make hard and fast business decisions. Harold Shaw tries to help the performer follow his or her own feelings. "If a performer has an artistic decision to make, I try to force that person to resolve it in their own mind. I always try to encourage an artist to go in the direction he has a natural bent to go in."

A manager is responsible for guiding an artist's career. This involves the very real problems of procuring enough work for the new artist to make a living. "The thing that most artists really want is a stack of contracts so that they'll be able to perform and make a living," Shaw observes. "This is difficult to accomplish when artist is first starting out. We need to establish a circuit for new recital artists. There should be an endowment so that young artists have the opportunity to play a series of 1,000 to 1,500 seat halls. England has such a system. But in America, it's tough to launch a new artist because the average 3,000 seat hall can get the best names."

Lifestyle

The successful manager is completely involved in his or her work. Harold Shaw's work day begins at 6:30 A.M. and ends at 1:00 A.M. During this time he is involved with activities that are work-related. His day might begin with an early breakfast with a business associate, while many of his evenings are spent attending concerts. But like most people in this profession, there is little separation between work, social life, and leisure time. "I don't really work," he explains. "I just live from the time I get up to the time I go to sleep. I don't consider that work."

ORCHESTRA ADMINISTRATION

Symphony orchestras have become large operations which require proper management. The budget for a medium-size orchestra like the Houston Philharmonic is currently over $6 million. Bigger orchestras like those in Chicago or Boston have budgets of over $15 million. As these operations grow, there is an increasing need for administrators with highly specialized skills. These administrators are responsible to the orchestra's executive director, who in turn must answer to a board of directors. Since most of the funding for a symphony orchestra is raised by contributions, an orchestra's board of directors is responsible to the community for how money is raised and spent.

The administrative staff of a large orchestra can run as high as fifty people. The executive director is responsible to the board of directors for all phases of the operation: Long-range planning; fund-raising and ticket sales; contract and labor negotiations; and staff supervision. The American Symphony Orchestra League is an organization that offers seminars and internships in orchestra management.

They describe some of the more prominent administrative positions in symphony orchestras as follows:

Assistant Manager—Sometimes called the operations manager or orchestra manager; functions directly below the executive director. Duties include supervision of administrative personnel, the coordination of repertoire, and the hiring of guest soloists and conductors.

Director of Development—Is responsible for planning and executing annual fund drives, preparing grant applications, and coordinating the activities of committees involved in fundraising.

Director of Public Relations—Promotes and publicizes the orchestra by writing and distributing press releases to the various print and broadcast media. This position involves presenting information about the orchestra's activities to the general public. Other duties may include editing and writing of program booklets and advertising copy.

Controller or Business Manager—Prepares budgets, financial statements, tax reports, account payments, and other financial business.

Director of Ticket Sales—Coordinates box office activities, ticket printing, and sales reports. Supervises the box office staff.

Today's symphony orchestras are multimillion dollar corporations. Ask people in the classical field, and they will tell you that good orchestra administrators are in great demand. As in any other complex business, an orchestra adminstrator must enter the field from his or her particular area of specialization. Two areas that have become increasingly important are fund-raising and marketing. But any area of orchestra management requires a sound background in business as well as an appreciation of classical music and the problems that musicians have to deal with.

Michael Wilcok, executive director and general manager of the Houston Philharmonic, sees a symphony orchestra as an important asset of the city in which it operates:

Every community supports its own orchestra. It's entirely up to the community in deciding how they want to run their orchestra. They raise the money. They buy the tickets. They make it happen. An orchestra should be an integral part of a city. It should be on a par with that city's baseball or football team. No better. But certainly no worse.

As general manager of a major symphony orchestra, it's my job to administer and distribute the funds that the community raises for its instrument. The funds are raised by volunteers in the community. My job is to work with them. I present plans and alternatives to use that money in the wisest fashion. I help the community develop their orchestra according to the resources they have available. I try to make it all happen by translating the community's efforts into tickets, a concert, and an audience.

Michael Wilcok On Becoming Executive Director of a Major Orchestra

My parents were good amateur musicians, but I never felt that I had the ability to be a performer. And I didn't want to teach because I didn't feel that I had the qualities that make a good teacher. So I decided to be someone who facilitated performances and helped other people perform. That side of the business really fascinated me.

I come from England, and I took my university training in music there. After graduation, I took a general traineeship working in an opera house. During this eighteen month program, you spend six weeks doing everything possible in an opera house. I spent six weeks in the box office, six weeks in the financial department, six weeks making scenery. I even spent six weeks selling ice cream. Gradually, I built up a jigsaw picture of the entire organization.

I was paid almost nothing and I sometimes became very discouraged. You were considered sweated labor with no position at all. People treated you as a goffer. They would constantly order you around. At times, it seemed as if they were trying to make things as difficult as possible. Actually, they were making sure you understood the realities of the business, not just the gloss on the surface. After my training, I became an assistant stage director with that same opera company.

I always had the desire to get into the record business. While I was working at the opera company, I wrote to all the record companies in London. One of them gave me an interview and said, "Don't call us, we'll call you." Six months later they called, and I got the job.

I spent the next eighteen years as a record producer for London Records. I liked the work. But I felt that I was working in an isolated situation. I decided that I wanted to get out of that and use what I had learned in a more practical way. I find that I enjoy being an (executive director). I feel that a good manager is a manipulator in the best sense of the word. I enjoy being able to manipulate all the resources—both the human and the financial resources—and get the best possible results out of all that.

Entering the Field of Classical Music Administration

Today's symphony orchestras are, in many ways, similar to corporations in other areas of business. The people who run orchestras have a strong knowledge of business as well as a love for music. Although there are only a limited number of positions available in symphony orchestras, capable and qualified people are in great demand. Michael Wilcok feels that a young person with an interest in the field will find a variety of roads to a career in orchestra administration.

There is no set formula for success in this field. In some areas of the corporate world there is a clearly defined path. People go to a particular school, take a particular course, and get a particular degree. In the field of music management, your experiences can come from a variety of points of view. This is such a broad field that people can enter it without any one particular set of qualifications. It is in the interests of the classical music business that we encourage as many people as possible to follow their own particular path into the field. . . .

Every orchestra manager you talk to will have a different kind of training. There's no set path and I don't think there should be. The things I do to run the orchestra in Houston probably wouldn't work in Pittsburgh or Chicago. A young person who feels that this is an area he wants to pursue will find a variety of ways to get involved.

Although there are a number of colleges offering degrees in music administration, professionals do not always agree on their value. However, nobody disputes the variety of opportunities that colleges and universities offer for aspiring administrators. Most colleges offer a series of classical music concerts that are handled by a local professional person in conjunction with a group of students. No matter what your major is, you can become involved with publicizing the events, or handling ticket sales, or working with the finance committee. By getting involved in these areas, a student can get a picture of what it takes to eventually become a successful administrator.

Sheldon Gold, president of ICM Artists, believes in a strong academic grounding in business subjects. While he holds a master's degree in business administration, he recognizes that a number of very successful managers and administrators have done quite well with much less formal education. Gold emphasizes the importance of specialization within the field:

The person graduating from school must decide which aspect of the business they want as their eventual goal. . . . This business has become much more complex in the past twenty years. We're talking about a major industry. If you're going to climb the ladder in this industry, you've got to be able to talk to a board of directors that is usually made up of the most successful business people in that community.... If you are the manager of a major performing arts center, you've got to be able to fill the stage with a compatible group of performing artists. You also must be able to negotiate with various unions, be it musicians, stagehands, or box office personnel. The executive director of the Metropolitan Opera has to deal with thirty-one separate unions. So if you are going to build a successful career, you better have the tools and the groundwork to deal with these complex problems.

Henry Fogel, orchestra manager of the New York Philharmonic, feels that a passionate love of music combined with good business sense can be more valuable than advanced degrees from a university.

I know it's very American to think that a college education is essential for a successful career, but I don't believe that. A broad background in liberal arts and business might be helpful. But I really feel that the practical experience and basic instinct are more important.... I dropped out of college after three and a half years because I had a chance to purchase my own radio station. I had been working at this small station in Syracuse, N.Y. while I was going to college there. Even then, I had a huge collection of classical records and I hosted the station's only classical music program. When the station went bankrupt, my friend and I bought it for one dollar.

When we took over the station we had to assume about fourteen thousand dollars in debts. I had to go to all the creditors and ask them to be patient.... But we built up the station and I ran it for fifteen years. During that time, I became a member of the board of directors of the Syracuse Symphony Orchestra. I was the first one to run a fund-raising radio marathon for a local symphony orchestra. Now they are held all over the country.... In 1978, I was recommended to the New York Philharmonic to help them run a fund-raising marathon on radio station WQXR. They liked my work and offered me the position I have now.

What Does it Take?

If you feel that you have a genuine interest in a career in arts administration, contact the American Symphony Orchestra League in Vienna, Virginia. They offer various seminars as well as a number of fellowships for promising individuals. Contact your local symphony orchestra and try to interview the general manager or another high level person. Henry Fogel tries to see one or two young people a month even if he has no jobs to give. He is always on the lookout for good people and gladly takes the time to help steer them in the right direction. These are some of the qualities he believes a good administrator should possess:

You must have the ability to work under pressure. There are many tensions involved with performing. Also, symphony orchestras are usually deficit operations, so they tend to be understaffed. This means that you must be willing to work far more than a normal 9-to-5 day. You must be able to deal with people—performing artists as well as business people. And you have to love music so that the tensions and pressures of the job are balanced by the satisfaction of listening to a concert and knowing that you helped make it happen. Other skills can be taught. But the ability to work under pressure, a lot of dedication, and a real belief in music are things you cannot learn. Either you have them or you don't. . . .

When you're ready to break into the field, you usually start out as a production assistant, press department assistant, or operations assistant. Then you have to do well to get noticed. This is a very small business. I like to say that if someone in the Syracuse Symphony sneezes, someone in the Denver Philharmonic will hand him a handkerchief. . . . So, it's a very closed field, and I'm always getting inquiries from other orchestras. If I know of a talented young person, I can sometimes help them find a position.

How Much Does it Pay?

Although high ranking people in orchestra management are well paid, they do not necessarily make as much money as people in similar positions in other businesses. "Most people don't enter this field for money," Henry Fogel points out.

> The New York Philharmonic is a $10 million a year corporation. I think that the top management officials of most other corporations of that size get paid significantly more money. The top paying music administration job ought to be the manager of a major opera company. Perhaps the top people in this field are just beginning to receive six-figure salaries.
>
> A friend of mine recently mentioned that he was upset about how much money sanitation men make. But what are the other rewards of that job? A person in a similar position to mine in an insurance company probably makes much more money than I do. But then again, who feels passionately about insurance? I realize that society probably needs sanitation or insurance more than it needs music. Medical care or legal help are probably more important than a symphony orchestra concert at any given moment. And that's how society rewards things. But I also deeply believe that a society also needs music as part of the cultrual heritage of mankind.

Outlook

The outlook for people wishing to pursue a career in arts management is quite good at this time. Although musicians are now being encouraged to become familiar with business subjects as an alternative in case performing does not work out, it is not necessary to have any formal music training to become a successful administrator. However, an understanding of the art form and an appreciation of the difficulties performers must face are an absolute must. One ultimate goal of all people involved with management and administration is to give the performers all the things they need to do their job. That's why one must understand everything that goes into a performance in order to be effective.

Although there is no prescription for success, a solid academic background in business and liberal arts is usually recommended. If your college gives a course in arts administration, you might find it useful, especially if professionals take part in the discussions. Henry Fogel feels that a major in arts administration is "overkill." However, he strongly recommends any of the intensive programs offered by the American Symphony Orchestra League. Any type of practical experience one can get in school—either through concert planning or internships—should be sought after.

Once an individual has laid the basic groundwork, chances of success are greatly improved by focusing on the specific type of work one wishes to become involved in. There are opportunities with orchestras, dance companies, and opera houses. There are specialists in public relations and music law. There are openings for general managers of large performing arts centers and for touring companies that travel all over the world. But whatever areas you choose, remember that you are dealing with an ever more complex field that demands business skill, a devotion to music, and a willingness to work extremely hard.

Additional Sources for Information About Careers in Classical Music

MUSICAL AMERICA ANNUAL—The Publishing House, Great Barrington, Massachusetts 01230

Offers a complete listing of orchestras, opera companies, festivals, music schools, contests, publishers, professional organizations, and magazines pertaining to the classical music field.

THE AMERICAN SYMPHONY ORCHESTRA LEAGUE—
P.O. Box 669, Vienna, Virgina 22180
A clearinghouse for information about symphony orchestras of all levels. Offers various seminars on the arts and arts administration. Publishes *Symphony News Magazine.*

NATIONAL ORCHESTRAL ASSOCIATION—111 W. 57th Street, New York, New York 10019
Activities include a training program for young musicians and composers who are about to embark on professional careers.

AMERICAN COMPOSERS ALLIANCE—170 W. 74th Street, New York, New York 10023
Handles licensing and performing rights for serious composers. It has an extensive musical library.

AMERICAN GUILD OF MUSICAL ARTISTS (AGMA)— 1841 Broadway, New York, New York 10023

Publications

INTERNATIONAL MUSICIAN—(220 Mount Pleasant Avenue, Newark, New Jersey 07104)

MUSICAL AMERICA—(1825 7th Avenue, New York, New York 10019)

OPERA NEWS—(1864 Broadway, New York, New York 10023)

CENTRAL OPERA SERVICE BULLETIN—(Metropolitian Opera, Lincoln Center Plaza, New York, New York 10023)

ORCHESTRA NEWS—(1729 Superior Avenue, Cleveland, Ohio 44114)

THE COMPOSER—(317 Nobel Drive, Santa Cruz, California 95060)

CHAPTER 4

Careers in Music Education

The development of tomorrow's great musicians and enthusiastic music lovers depends on the dedication and skill of music educators on all levels. An innovative music teacher in elementary school can give a child a love for music that will last a lifetime. A gifted high school band director who truly loves his work conveys a spirit of teamwork that students carry with them into every phase of activity. A patient and caring private teacher can motivate students to make music a permanent part of their lives.

There is a saying that, "Those who can, do, and those who can't, teach." But surely this applies only to bad teachers who are not going to make a real difference in their students' lives. Teaching is, in fact, a rare gift that has always been undervalued in our society. In most communities sanitation men earn more money than teachers. Professional athletes and rock stars can make more money in a single

154

week than an experienced teacher earns in an entire year. But few people are so vital to our society as the gifted and dedicated educator.

In the past, a number of people sought careers in teaching as a last resort. If the thing they really wanted to do with their life did not turn out, they could always turn to teaching. On the surface, there are many attractions to the life of an educator. The working day is traditionally shorter than the nine-to-five hours that most people have to deal with. The vacation time is extraordinary. Summers off, a week for Christmas, another week for Easter, and many other holidays. But, in fact, a good teacher works extremely hard for relatively little money and even less respect from the general public. However, for those individuals who genuinely love to teach and live for the excitement and satisfaction of helping to shape young minds, no other work is as rewarding.

In today's tight job market, teachers are no longer in great demand. A person seeking a career in music education has to realize that jobs are far less plentiful than they once were. The outlook at this writing is fairly grim. When a school district cuts its budget, music is usually one of the first subject areas to suffer. The people seeking a career in music education must be individuals who really want it. They are probably going to have to extend their studies well beyond a four-year college degree to have a chance at one of the few available positions. Most teachers of elementary and high school music now have master's degrees. With only a few exceptions, colleges want their professors to have Ph.D.'s. After all the time and money spent on obtaining degrees, one must face the real possibility of not finding a job.

As competitive as the field of music education has become, there will always be some openings for the right candidates. But this has now become a field for those who

FACT SHEET
CAREERS IN MUSIC EDUCATION

Career	Opportunities for Employment	Education and Training	Skills and Personality Traits
MUSIC TEACHER IN A SCHOOL SETTING	• Elementary, Junior High, High School • Instrumental • General Music • Band, Orchestra • Choral Director	• College degree in music education • Master's degree necessary in some districts • Licensing as per state requirements	• Love of children • Ability to relate to age level that one teaches • Musical talent • Working knowledge of several instruments • Patience • Knowledge of instrumental and choral literature
COLLEGE AND CONSERVATORY TEACHER	•2- and 4-year colleges and universities and conservatories—teaching general music and/or specific areas of specialization such as composition, history, or applied studies	• Ph.D. required for most college teaching positions • Well-known performers without advanced degrees teach special classes	• Basic teaching skills • Ability to communicate to large classes, small seminars, and individual students • Strong research and writing skills necessary for advancement in most universities • Strong musical background in both theory and performance

Lifestyle	Earnings	Employment Outlook
• Short hours • Good vacations and benefits • Much preparation needed to be a truely effective teacher • Job security after tenure	• Average salary for 10-month year approx. $15,000	• Very tight job market • Very few openings • Relocation might be necessary to find position
• Short hours • Good vacations and benefits • Many hours spent in libraries and archives gathering research and writing it up in publishable form • Job security after tenure	• Approx. $15,000– $40,000 depending on experience, status, and institution in which one is employed	• Keen competition • Many more qualified applicants than job openings • Extremely difficult to get tenure

FACT SHEET
CAREERS IN MUSIC EDUCATION

Career	Opportunities for Employment	Education and Training	Skills and Personality Traits
PRIVATE TEACHER	• Music studios • Private music schools • Private practice	• No formal educational requirements • No state or federal agencies that license and oversee the activities of private music schools or teachers	• Mastery of vocal skills or musical instrument(s) that one is teaching • Solid musical background and performing experience • Patience • Business skills
MUSIC THERAPIST	• Hospitals • Clinics for handicapped children • Corrective institutions • Special education facilities • College teacher of music therapy	• Bachelor's degree in music therapy required • Master's degree desirable	• Ability to play several instruments including piano and guitar • Ability to work with people who have special needs and problems • Some choral and instrumental conducting skills

regard it as their first choice. You ought to be willing to accept a position in any geographic area where one becomes available. You must develop musical, educational, and job hunting skills in order to keep a leg up on the competition. If you do decide that a career in music education is for you, there are a variety of positions to consider. *The Music Educators National Conference* (MENC) has compiled this comprehensive list of job titles in music education:

Lifestyle	Earnings	Employment Outlook
• Irregular hours, nights and weekends • Some traveling • Seasonal work • Subject to cancellation on short notice	• From $5 to $50 per lesson, depending on instrument, qualifications, and geographical area • Competition • Most people do not base their entire income on private teaching	• These services will always be in demand • Success as a private teacher depends on versatility, advertising, public relations skills, and recommendations of former students
• Therapists in hospital settings expected to involve the patients in extra activities outside of normal working hours • In school settings lifestyle is much like that of a teacher	• Low to moderate • Approx. $8,000–$15,000 • Similar to teacher's salary scale	• Fairly good at this time, especially for those who are willing to take any kind of job opening in whatever geographic area they become available • As the possibilities in this field expand, there is a growing demand for music therapists to give private sessions outside of institutional settings

Instrumental music teacher; elementary and junior high school general music teacher; junior high school band, orchestra, or chorus director; senior high school band, orchestra, or chorus director; senior high school specialist in general music, music literature, music theory, and allied arts; secondary school instrumental music lab specialist; college, university, or conservatory music teacher (in education, history and literature, theory and composition, performance, applied study, etc.); music education researcher; university music administrator; studio or private music teacher; performance coach; government arts education consultant, supervisor, or administrator; freelance clinician and lecturer; and music industry educational consultant.

TEACHING MUSIC IN THE ELEMENTARY SCHOOL

One reason it is difficult to find that first teaching position is because of a system called tenure. This basically means that a teacher on any level who has been at his or her job for a certain number of years is guaranteed job security for life. Because of the scarcity of job opportunities, people will rarely leave their positions once they receive tenure. This can be unfortunate if the tenured person is not a particularly good teacher.

Many students get out of school without a knowledge and appreciation of music because they never received the right kind of exposure. Patricia Sohn, an experienced elementary and junior high school music teacher, blames this situation on the unfocused music education programs that are all too common in our schools.

I've met a lot of music teachers who are just biding time. Their skills are appalling. Many of them can't even play piano, which is the most basic skill in elementary school music teaching. Other teachers don't want to teach skills. They want to do the so-called fun things and their programs become very unstructured. Their classes tend to degenerate into film showing and record playing. One school I know of had a tremendous amount of money for their music program and the teacher could have done anything she wanted. But her idea of music education was handing out the lyrics of popular songs to the kids and having them sing for forty-five minutes. The point is that instead of looking at music, these kids are looking at words.

My focus as an elementary school music teacher is stressing skills. I teach my students music-reading and singing skills. I also do some things they consider fun, like making musical instruments, creative movement, and talking about composers. I contend that children can appreciate music only in so far as they have a working knowledge of the language of music. Otherwise, they are quite limited. You can play beautiful music for your classes all day and point out the expressive qualities of that music. But unless they can dig in and do some of it themselves, they are not really learning music.

Patricia Sohn recognizes the need for new young music teachers who are dedicated and creative. But she realizes that it is difficult to bring new people into school systems that are constantly trying to cut their budgets. She candidly cites poor teaching as a major reason why music programs are often among the first in line to feel the heavy axe of budget cuts.

The reason for many music programs going down the drain is that parents often aren't excited enough about what their kids are doing and the teachers themselves are usually responsible for that. I believe in having parents come into the classroom to see what I'm doing. After all, it's their taxes that pay for teachers' salaries. . . . But many music programs are wishy-washy and the kids go home and tell their parents: "Oh, we sang this and we listened to that." The parents can tell that nothing very exciting is going on. No wonder they feel that they can do without music programs.

Qualities of a Good Music Teacher

"The most important quality is a real enthusiasm for what you're doing," says Patricia Sohn.

Kids know if you're bored or if you love your work. If you really love your work, they will catch some of that enthusiasm and respond. You must also be able to relate to the age level

Music teacher Patricia Sohn instructing a class.

that you work with. If you hate teenagers, you're going to have a rough time in a high school. You have to believe that what you are doing is very important or you will never be any good. A teacher must have the welfare of the child uppermost in his or her mind at all times. Kids can become very turned off if the attitude of a teacher is belligerent or not compassionate to their particular learning difficulty. . . .

Kids sometimes think they can't sing because their mothers or fathers told them to shut up and now they won't sing again. A lot of kids can hear, but they just don't know what to do with their throats. So you have to work with each child individually in a very methodical way. . . . If a kid decides to learn an instrument, you have to make them understand that it's a discipline just like spelling or math. Kids often see music as something that's fun and comes naturally, but you've got to make them understand that they are going to have to work very hard in order to master an instrument.

PRIVATE TEACHING

The same basic qualities that would make a person effective teaching groups of students at a particular age level in a school setting would also apply to individuals who teach privately or in music studios. Patricia Sohn views private teaching as an ideal situation. "Someone is paying you to sit down for an hour and work one to one. The whole private student relationship is a lot more efficient because you are focusing on the abilities of that one student."

In spite of its advantages, there are a few problems that are peculiar to private music teachers. In the first place, the students are not graded as they are in a school setting, so it is sometimes more difficult to get them to practice. The relationship between private student and teacher is often more intimate and friendly than in school situations. This can be a great advantage. But at times, the student might

The author working with a guitar student.

feel that if he or she does not practice, there is not much the teacher can do. Also, since the private teacher is often paid by the individual lesson, he or she must sometimes weigh the student's talent and progress against financial considerations. But the teacher who can somehow motivate students to practice holds the real key to success.

"The best teacher is one who can inspire the student to practice and work more on his own," says violinist Sung Rai Sohn. "Preparation on the part of the student is the main thing, whether you're teaching little kids or advanced college students. The best teachers don't dictate. Instead, they give the students more information so that they will want to do the work on their own."

Do great musicians always make the best teachers? "Not necessarily," says Sung Rai Sohn, an accomplished musician and highly regarded teacher in his own right.

> Great players are sometimes so much into their own playing, their own technique, and their own ideas that they ignore the needs of their students. I once had a problem like that with my own teacher. My teacher was tall and had long hands. He put a great deal of pressure on me because I was smaller physically and couldn't hold the violin the same way as he did.
>
> The best teachers can adjust to the individual problems of their students. In a way, you're like a doctor. You must solve your students' problems right away or they will get worse. If you don't solve problems, then you're not a very good teacher.

While Sung Rai Sohn teaches master classes in violin to advanced students at Sarah Lawrence College, his wife Patricia gives piano lessons to elementary and high school students who wish to study privately. In spite of the differences in the age and abilities of their students, they both agree on the basic qualities that a good private teacher should possess.

"One of the most important qualities of a good teacher is an enormous amount of patience," says Patricia Sohn. There is a world of difference between a teacher who is bored and passive and one who truly has patience:

> One needs a reactive kind of patience which lets you listen very hard to what a child is trying to get out and then assess it. You've got to figure out why they haven't caught on to what you've said when you have repeated that same thing five times in the last five minutes. You have to find out why that isn't sinking in and try to work it through.
>
> Some teachers have a short fuse and get angry at their students. But once a teacher shows his or her frustration, everything shuts down and there is no learning. If you can keep yourself relaxed, even if the student isn't doing what you want, that's an important key.

There are many techniques a teacher can use to motivate his or her student. Many younger students come into their first guitar lesson and ask when they will be able to play as well as Eric Clapton. It is the job of the teacher to point out that nobody becomes a skilled player without putting in a good deal of time. If one can instill in one's students the desire to play well and the motivation to practice in a disciplined and consistent way, that teacher has won 90 percent of the battle.

TEACHING MUSIC IN THE HIGH SCHOOL

If a talented student has the right kind of training in elementary and junior high school, there are many exciting possibilities for the high school music teacher to explore. This is especially true at a place like New York City's High School of Performing Arts. The excitement of working with the most gifted and motivated young musicians in that city is reflected in the atmosphere of Gabriel Kosakoff's fifth-floor office in this ancient school building in the middle of Broadway's theatre district.

Mr. Kosakoff is more than happy to talk about his work as a music educator. But as chairman of the Performing Arts music department, he continues to do that work even as he discusses it. The band is practicing next door, and it is difficult to carry on a conversation. But Mr. Kosakoff is completely at ease with all of the noise. Now and then a student will walk in and ask him to sign something. There is a quality about the way he deals with the students that tells you that you are in the presence of a man who truly loves his work.

Like many of his colleagues in the field of music education, Kosakoff set out to become a professional musician. But he is extremely happy working with high school students and has no regrets.

Gabriel Kosakoff conducts the All City High School Band in their annual performance on the steps of New York's City Hall.

I actually feel fortunate that I wasn't good enough to make it as a professional trombone player. . . . I have so many friends that are talented musicians who come to me asking for teaching jobs. Some of them are such good players that I wish I could study with them myself. But I have no jobs for them. I'm lucky to have my job. . . . I have also found that the best players don't always make the best teachers. Those who look at music education as something to do if they can't make it as musicians sometimes project that attitude in the classroom.

Because the students at the High School of Performing Arts are among the most talented in the New York City area, a number of them will go on to become professionals. Others soon find out that they might not be as exceptional on their instruments as they once believed. "Almost every kid that comes here is the top musician in his junior high school," says Kosakoff. "But when they get here, everybody is a good player, and it's sometimes a rude awakening when they find themselves playing third clarinet."

The curriculum at Performing Arts is geared to give students the skills they will need to compete as professionals. Kosakoff continues:

A musician is like an athlete in that he must prove himself every day. Everything depends not just on how good you are, but on how good you are that day. . . . We make our students perform at least once a week in front of their classes. Then, the class members will critically compare that performance to previous performances. . . . Each student must also play several times a year for the faculty, so that each student who gets out of here exposes himself as a solo performer constantly. If they don't do well, most of them will go home and practice harder. And those who find this experience to be a painful process are also learning something about themselves.

Because of the tremendous competition, a large number of Performing Arts graduates will not be able to make a living as performers. That is why teachers stress experiences that will help students in all phases of their lives. Performing well at auditions, for example, teaches individuals to keep their heads in all kinds of pressure situations. Mastering an instrument creates an atmosphere of work discipline that serves people well in any kind of career.

But the most important benefit of music education as a high school student might be the experience one acquires in getting along with others. This is especially true for students who participate in the school chorus, band, or orchestra.

"Music is the art of teamwork," says Gabriel Kosakoff. "We spend a lot of time teaching teamwork to our students. If you hit a wrong note at an audition, you fail. But if you hit a wrong note in an orchestra, the orchestra fails. Every individual has a responsibility to society and that's what music education is really about."

MUSIC CONSERVATORIES

Conservatories are the most important breeding grounds for aspiring classical musicians. Indeed, many conservatory students are already earning substantial amounts of money as professional musicians while they are completing their courses. Although conservatories do have academic requirements, the greater emphasis is on preparing a student to function as a professional. Peter Mennin, president of The Juilliard School, candidly admits that if a student is talented enough, academic deficiencies will not hold him back. But Elliott Galkin, president of the Peabody Conservatory in Baltimore, has a different point of view:

> The days of the conservatory when the musician was trained to play his fiddle to perform before the public are long gone. The conservatory now has a responsibility to recognize that any education, no matter how technical, must be emerged in

the general culture. We cannot afford to develop musicians . . .
who are magnificent technicians (with) limited interests. Musicians who are being educated that way are being short-
changed.

Administrators of conservatories also have differing
views on the amount of time that ought to be devoted to
preparing students for alternate careers in music-related
areas. Some point out that any time spent in a course such
as music administration would allow that much less time
for the student to practice and perfect his or her musician-
ship. But others recognize that many graduates of even the
finest conservatories will not be able to make an adequate
living as a performer. They also feel that even people who
are lucky enough to become featured soloists or major conductors would profit greatly by having some understanding
about the business side of music.

Administrating a Conservatory

Unlike their colleagues in elementary and high schools,
most college and conservatory professors have no specific
training in education or administration. Peter Mennin feels
strongly about the kind of background a person needs to
be an effective administrator at a place like Juilliard. "To
have my job, you have to know how to make artistic
policy. There is a big difference between those who make
policy and those who carry it out. You can be the head of a
place like Juilliard with no administrative training or experience."

A good administrator without the right kind of artistic
background would flop at a place like Peabody or Juilliard.
When you are dealing with conductors and musicians, they
are not going to respond to your policies unless you are a
professional yourself. One acquires the administrative
skills on the job. But at a normal university, one's administrative skills are far more important than at a conservatory.

Working with Students

Conservatory students have already accomplished a great deal on their instruments. But the question of whether they will become successful professionals may not be answered for some time. One of the conservatory's main functions is to help students make the transition from gifted young musicians to professional performing artists. Peabody's Elliott Galkin tries to expose his students to many different aspects of what a successful performer needs to make a life in today's complex music world.

> We have all kinds of individuals speaking to students to try to show them that the life of a twentieth century musician is a very complicated and very difficult one. The students know that to be a star is going to be very, very difficult. At the same time, those students who are (filled) with the desire to be professional musicians will not be dissuaded. You cannot say to them, "It's tough out there. And the number of people who become piano soloists or violin soloists is very limited indeed." They won't take it. They are sure that they are going to be among those limited few.

People like Galkin and Mennin find working with gifted young musicians to be a satisfying and rewarding career. They both have time to pursue other musical interests, but they recognize that the development of tomorrow's great performers is a vital contribution in any art. "The real joy of teaching," Mennin observes, "is when you have a hungry, talented artist that wants to learn."

COLLEGE AND UNIVERSITY TEACHING

The teacher in a college or university setting usually has to work with non-music majors who take a required music course in addition to students who are specializing in some area of music. After a number of years, the college music professor might get to spend most or all of his or her time working in an area of specialization. Perhaps the teaching of required music courses to non-music majors would be more rewarding if teachers in the earlier grades had provided their students with a stronger foundation. But all too often, the college teacher has to cover ground that has been neglected at the lower educational levels.

Still, there is a great challenge in developing an interest in music in people who are either indifferent to music or else turned off by their previous courses. The college music teacher is often the last person who will have the opportunity to instill a love of music in many students. How is this best accomplished?

"The main idea is to get students to listen to music," says Allan Atlas, a full professor of music at Brooklyn College.

> I try to point out the basic things one should listen for. I try to teach the differences between the various styles and get them to understand the differences between a concerto and a symphony. What a general music course shouldn't be is a dry discussion of music history. This turns students off immediately. I rarely mention dates or give biographical facts, other than an anecdote or two. I basically make it a course on how to listen to music. I start with the assumption that a composer does things in a rational way, and we take a look at the things that a composer does from that point of view.

It is interesting to note that most teachers of general music courses on all levels claim to have quite a bit of latitude in what they teach. But because there is not much standardization of the skills people learn, the college teacher can only build on the abilities the students have already acquired. Allan Atlas finds that a good general music course on the college level will often stimulate students to take other music electives that are geared especially for non-music majors. In fact, he points to the enrollment in such electives as a good way to judge the effectiveness of a basic music course and the professor who is teaching it.

Breaking Into the Field

The job opportunities for a qualified person attempting to find his or her first college teaching position are very scarce. "In order to get a job in today's tight market," counsels Allan Atlas, "you will probably have to be willing to go out into the 'sticks.' You will certainly have to go outside of the small circle of prestigious schools. . . . But even at the worst school in the middle of nowhere, there might be 200 applicants for a single position. . . . There are simply too many applicants for the number of jobs. And you could safely say that nobody is desperate for music professors. I know many people who give up after awhile and change careers. Still, I would say that half of our Ph.D. graduates who are looking for positions do find them."

Most college professors have Ph.D.'s in a particular specialization area within music. Allan Atlas is a music historian who specializes in fifteenth century opera. Like most of his colleagues, Atlas has strong musical skills and an undergraduate degree from a liberal arts college.

Almost every professor I know in the City University of New York (CUNY) system is a good musician with a solid musical background. Most of them chose a liberal arts college over a conservatory because they wanted more academic background than a conservatory could offer. I don't know any university teachers who have taken education courses, and I doubt that these courses would help one become a better college teacher. Most college teachers take Ph.D.'s in their area of specialization and instinctively pick up the techniques of teaching by working in classroom situations.

Allan Atlas was appointed to the Brooklyn College staff in 1971. Although the job market is considerably tighter now, the procedures for finding that first position are very much the same. Here are the steps that Professor Atlas took in order to find his job:

> During the year I finished my doctoral dissertation, I sent out about forty applications. Some schools never answered at all. But I did get about six or seven responses. In several of those cases, the opportunities disappeared because of budget cuts or other reasons. I had three schools considering me when I got a call from Brooklyn College. They said, "We have an opening. Can you come for an interview?" I was interviewed by a five-person committee which is called the department of applications committee. They asked me a whole bunch of questions. I also had to submit letters of recommendation. They very next day, they called me up to tell me I had the job.

Qualities of a Good College Teacher

"You have to like teaching and you have to like doing research," says Allan Atlas.

> In order to do research, you have to spend a lot of time in libraries, archives, and places like that. If either the solitary work of doing research, the public work of lecturing in front of a class of thirty students in a low-level undergraduate class, or the more intensive teaching of five students in a Ph.D. seminar doesn't appeal to you, academic life probably isn't for you. If you are the kind of person who feels inhibited talking in front of thirty or forty people, you are not going to become a successful teacher. You might be a wonderful researcher, but when you get into the classroom you're going to die.

People who desire to make a life in the academic world must somehow balance the demands of being a good researcher with the energies that are needed for effective teaching. Allan Atlas sees no contradiction in these qualities. "The people who are the leading researchers are generally also very good teachers. And the good teachers also tend to do good research. The two qualities seem to go hand-in-hand. I can think of very few people who use their research as an excuse for not preparing classes."

Moving Up the Ladder

When a person is hired for the first teaching job, she is most often given the title of assistant professor. After a number of years, she is promoted to associate professor and given tenure. This means that she now has lifetime job security and can only be fired under very unusual circumstances. On the other hand, if the assistant professor does not receive tenure after a specified period of time, that individual will be dropped from the faculty.

There are sometimes rumblings that people are denied tenure because the school would rather hire a new teacher and pay him or her a lower salary. However, Professor Atlas denies that such manipulations take place at CUNY.

> Tenure is denied on three grounds: (1) The person hasn't published much and has not made a name for themselves as a scholar; (2) The person's teaching skills were mediocre and remained mediocre after a number of years; (3) The word comes down from the president or the dean that says, "We're very sorry but we have to cut three people from your department."
>
> You cannot cut a tenured person. But if you have a person coming up for tenure who is very weak and a stronger teacher who is three or four years away from tenure, you go with the stronger person. And you hope that by the time the stronger person comes up for tenure, you will be able to find a place for him.

The saying "publish or perish" is commonly used when people discuss getting ahead in the academic world. The lack of research by a particular department in a university reflects on the reputation of that institution. Universities want professors who are going to be able to make a name for themselves in the academic world. "It's true that a professor's main salary is paid because that person is teaching," says Allan Atlas, "but you are also supposed to be a scholar and you should publish."

I think that the more research you do the better teacher you will be. If you don't do research, you're going to wind up stagnating as a teacher. You don't have to do much research to teach a freshman music course. But if you are going to teach well on the graduate level, you must do research in order to stimulate both yourself and your students. So I think that the pressure to publish is basically a positive one.

If you've been at a school for five or six years and you're coming up for tenure, you can figure that you will be denied tenure if you haven't been published. Once you get tenured and become an associate professor, you have to continue publishing if you want to become a full professor. Once you make tenure and become an associate professor, the problem of job security no longer exists. Once you become a full professor, the incentive of promotions is no longer there. But you might want to transfer to a better university at some point, and you can only keep in the forefront by publishing. . . . I still publish because I enjoy it and I also believe that it is an important part of what a scholar does.

Lifestyle and Money

For the person who thrives on the various aspects of teaching and researching, the life of a college professor can be very rewarding. The dedicated professor often finds that the rewards become greater with time. After ten years in the CUNY system, Professor Atlas spends most of his teaching time working with Ph.D. students in his area of specialization. He feels lucky to be able to do work that he really cares about. "Most people who end up in this career really enjoy it," Atlas observes. "I enjoy teaching and I am still very much involved with writing articles for scholarly journals. I also get grants to go to Europe during the summer and do research. So I am quite happy with my work and I think most of my colleagues feel the same way."

The salary for a college professor varies tremendously, depending on the school and the particular step a person is on. The salary for an assistant professor just starting out in the CUNY system is around $16,000. A full professor at the top of that scale currently makes about $42,000. The salary range for professors at CUNY is probably somewhat higher than the national average, but these figures are a good guide to the vast differences between income levels at both ends of the scale.

MUSIC THERAPY

Richard Graham, president of the *National Association for Music Therapy* (NAMT), defines a music therapist as follows:

> A music specialist who uses music in the therapy of human disabilities. Music therapists are most likely to be located in settings that normally employ other members of the helping professions such as physicians, clinical psychologists, social workers, and rehabilitation specialists. In these settings, music therapists work either as team members or individually to assist their clientele to become healed, rehabilitated, or specially educated. Most music therapists do their work in mental hospitals, training centers for the developmentally disabled, rehabilitation centers, and—to a lesser extent—elementary and secondary school settings.

In order to be an approved NAMT therapist, an individual must pursue a course of study at an approved university. These studies are generally included in a school's music education department. The curriculum includes basic courses in music and music education, psychology, sociology, and clinical experience. Many music therapists find it useful to obtain a master's degree. But there are also some effective people in the field who have never had any formal training in music therapy.

Music can be a positive tool in helping people express their emotions. Effective music therapists can sometimes reach a disturbed patient through music after all else has failed. Emotionally disturbed children are sometimes greatly aided by music therapy, as are the retarded. The work can be rewarding to a person who is comfortable working with people who have various psychological and emotional problems. Furthermore, there seem to be job openings for graduates of qualified programs, particularly in hospitals. But the pay is quite low and the work one does is often overlooked.

A psychiatrist who teaches a course for music therapists at New York University describes the status of a music therapist in the hierarchy of hospital personnel this way: "The doctors have the most status. Then come the nurses. Then come people like psychiatric social workers. Then come the orderlies. And the music therapist is beneath all of them."

Of course, there have been a number of exceptional people who have gained tremendous respect on their hospital staffs for the wonderful work they have done. But there are also many hospital settings in which the music therapist spends the bulk of his or her time conducting sing-alongs with the patients. This is all well and good. But the therapist who has spent a good deal of time and money on schooling must find these situations distressing.

The situation in special schools for emotionally disturbed or retarded children is somewhat better. The techniques of music therapy seem to work rather well with these children. The work tends to be more specialized, and the therapists are looked upon with more respect in these settings. If one can get a position within a public school system, the salaries can easily surpass those in a hospital.

The career of music therapist is recommended for people who genuinely want to help others without any great returns in status or salary. There are likely to be jobs available in this field, particularly for those who are willing to relocate in an area where an opening exists. A competent music therapist should have adequate performance skills on a number of instruments. But perhaps the most important quality is the ability to communicate with others and help them become healthier human beings.

Additional Sources for Information About Careers in Music Education

MUSIC EDUCATORS NATIONAL CONFERENCE (MENC)—1902 Association Drive, Reston, Virginia 22091

Represents 64,000 music educators, prospective music educators, and others interested in music education at all levels. It sponsors various conventions and publishes *The Music Educators Journal.*

ASSOCIATION OF COLLEGE, UNIVERSITY AND COMMUNITY ARTS ADMINISTRATORS—Box 2137, Madison, Wisconsin 53701

NATIONAL ASSOCIATION OF SCHOOLS OF MUSIC— 11250 Royal Bacon Drive, #5, Reston, Virginia 22090

NATIONAL ASSOCIATION FOR MUSIC THERAPY (NAMT)—P.O. Box 610, Lawrence, Kansas 66044

Included in its many functions is the publication of *The Journal of Music Therapy.*

NATIONAL ASSOCIATION OF TEACHERS OF SINGING—250 W. 57th Street, New York, New York 10019

AMERICAN MUSIC CONFERENCE—150 E. Huron Street, Chicago, Illinois 60611

Publications

THE AMERICAN MUSIC TEACHER—(Music Teachers National Association, 408 Carew Tower, Cincinnati, Ohio 45202)

JOURNAL OF THE AMERICAN MUSICOLOGICAL SOCIETY—(201 South 34th Street, Philadelphia, Pennsylvania 19174)

MUSIC AMERICA—(P.O. Box 1852, 1320 Pearl Street, Boulder, Colorado 80306)
     Instructional articles for educators and students.

ETHNOMUSICOLOGY—(Society for Ethnomusicology, Room 513, 210 South Main Street, Ann Arbor, Michigan 48104)

THE INSTRUMENTALIST—(1418 Lake Street, Evanston, Illinois 60201)

CHAPTER 5

Writing and Journalism Careers in Music

There are a number of career opportunities for people who wish to combine their love for music with an ability to write. Music critics and reporters are probably the most visible people who write about music. But there are also publicity writers, magazine editors, liner-note writers, program annotators, and music historians. Many people who write about music find it necessary or desirable to combine two or more of these areas. The various careers need different skills. But all music writing careers require a thorough understanding of the kind(s) of music you are talking about and strong writing skills.

FACT SHEET
WRITING AND JOURNALISM CAREERS

Career	Opportunities for Employment	Education and Training	Skills and Personality Traits
CRITIC (Classical, jazz, rock and pop)	• Newspapers • Magazines • Radio and television stations • Speciality and trade publications	• Formal music education is desirable for classical and jazz criticism • Many rock critics have no formal music background • College degree recommended, courses in music, journalism, language, business, and psychology	• Solid background in music • Understanding of the musical style(s) one is writing about • Good writing, research, and interview skills
MUSIC REPORTER AND/OR HISTORIAN	• Same as critic • Most music writiers do both reporting and criticism • This work can sometimes generate material for books	SAME AS CRITIC	SAME AS CRITIC
MUSIC PUBLICATIONS EDITING	SAME AS CRITIC	• College degree with emphasis on journalism and writing courses	• Knowledge of editing and mechanics of printing and publishing • Knowledge of music helpful but often less important than editing and journalistic skills

Lifestyle	Earnings	Employment Outlook
• Night and weekend work • Pressure of working under deadlines • Fringe benefits such as free tickets, records, and invitations to openings	• Moderate to good for the few full-time critics on major newspapers or magazines • Variable fees and irregular work schedule for freelancers	• Poor for anyone thinking of music criticism as a full-time career • Many more openings for those willing to do occasional freelance pieces
SAME AS CRITIC	SAME AS CRITIC	SAME AS CRITIC
• Regular working hours • Extra work and pressures on deadline days • Some music editors do freelance reporting and criticism	• Moderate income level possible at more established publications • Starting salaries are generally low	• Highly competitive • There is very little turnover at the better publications

FACT SHEET
WRITING AND JOURNALISM CAREERS

Career	Opportunities for Employment	Education and Training	Skills and Personality Traits
PUBLIC RELATIONS WRITING	• Established public relations firms • Record companies • Publishing houses • Your own business	• College degree recommended, courses include journalism, music, and business	• Strong writing skills • Ability to deal with all kinds of people • Salesmanship • Strong knowledge of the musical field one is operating in • Ability to establish and maintain contacts

CLASSICAL MUSIC CRITIC, REPORTER, HISTORIAN

Virgil Thomson, the esteemed classical music composer and critic, once said: "The concert doesn't finish with the last downbeat. The concert finishes with the last period that the critic places on his article about that downbeat." Is criticism really that important? If you consider the number of people who might read a review of a concert compared to the number of people who actually attended that concert, you begin to get an idea of the kind of influence a critic might have. If you read an excellent review of a particular conductor, or singer, or soloist, you might make it a point to attend that artist's next concert. Or you might go out and buy that performer's latest record. From this point of view, it is easy to see how an accumulation of good reviews can launch a performer to the top of his or her field. At the

Lifestyle	Earnings	Employment Outlook
• Night and weekend work often required • Mixing social life with business	• Very lucrative for top independent press agents • Good for people working with established firms	• Very competitive in rock and pop music • More openings for those with skills in the classical music field

same time, enough "bad press" has ruined many promising careers.

All of this has left artists with an interesting point of view about critics. Good performers want to know how their work comes across. They are also interested in positive and constructive criticism on how they can improve. But a classical performer who has put in years of practice and preparation expects no less of the critic who passes judgment on his work. And rightfully so.

Music critic and educator Elliot Galkin strongly agrees with the school of thought that a good critic is a musician who can write. He suggests that a five or six year program be developed to train people in the necessary music and writing skills. "Perhaps then they will be able to write with compassion. Without an understanding of what it takes to put on a great performance, one cannot write with compassion. But a well-trained, compassionate critic is important to both performers and audiences. The act of writing a review is to continue the concert past those who heard it to those who didn't hear it," Galkin observes. "Critics are the educators of the public and they can contribute a positive roll."

Shirley Flemming, classical music critic for the *New York Post,* does not believe that a critic must necessarily label a performance either *good* or *bad:*

> I don't sit down with the idea of passing judgment on how the San Francisco orchestra played Beethoven's Fifth Symphony. . . . You sort of sit down and explain how it was and how it differed from other performances. By the time you finish doing that, your viewpoint on whether it was good or left something to be desired kind of expresses itself. I like to think of it more as an explanation than a judgment. I think a critic should try to make a reader interested so they'll say, "Next time, maybe I ought to go."

Education and Training

Shirley Flemming, like most competent classical music critics, has an extensive background in music.

> I majored in classical music in college and then got a master's in musicology. There probably are a few critics who learned from going to concerts and listening to records. But for me, studying music and playing an instrument have been very helpful. You look at music and musicians in a different way. . . . I've played in my college orchestra and in a semi-professional orchestra and that is invaluable. Nothing teaches you how to listen to an orchestra like playing in an orchestra. . . .
>
> Someone who is dedicated enough could give themselves a good education by going to concerts and listening to records. But you have to know how to read scores, and you will need some outside instruction for that. . . . I must admit that I am a little skeptical of critics who have never played anything themselves. It is disturbing to a musician that people are just sitting on the sidelines picking out things to criticize when they really don't know that much about it.

Shirley Flemming points to the Music Critics Association of America as an organization that offers seminars and other programs for young critics. Thomas Willis, music critic of the *Chicago Tribune,* points out that there is no one way to train. "Heaven help us if all critics came through one course or curriculum or were accredited by one board or committee. We need many different writers, each with his own contributions to make." Aside from extensive professional training in music and attending a university near a large cultural complex, Willis suggests that aspiring music critics would benefit from studying the following subjects:

> Music theory and history develop the long view and are an absolute necessity in assessing the (work) of new composers and performers. . . . General studies, acoustics, four or five foreign languages, courses in other related arts, and a seminar or two in communication psychology would all be useful in today's rapidly changing arts world. . . . Elementary management training, computer science, and "human engineering" wouldn't hurt either. . . .

Breaking into the Field

Like any other writing profession, the first step for the young music critic is to get published. You can do that by submitting articles or ideas to school and local newspapers. No matter how talented you are, you must be prepared to deal with a great deal of rejection. Also, do not even think about making a reasonable fee for your work when you start out. However, a few good published pieces in your college or local paper can soon lead to bigger and better things. You would be wise to not limit your scope to music criticism alone. There are very few writers who earn their living writing only music criticism. Thomas Willis spent years writing about theatre and films before becoming a full-time music critic. Shirley Flemming works as an editor at *Musical America* and does music criticism only on weekday evenings. So if you want to make a career writing about music, be as versatile as you can.

Sylvia Kraft, press and promotion manager at Schirmer Music, poses a number of useful suggestions for the young writer:

> You can start making a name for yourself while you're still in school. If a familiar artist comes to play at your school, try to interview him. Don't ask him why he is so famous. Instead, ask him why he takes the time to come to a school. Ask what advice he can impart to students. This can be a new approach to a famous person. People are interested in the things great artists do aside from concert hall performances. Write the interview up and try to sell it.
>
> There are many things a young person can do on their own. Read as many music publications as you can. See what kind of stories they run and how they are written. Think of a story you want to write and then go out and sell it. Contact different editors. Be aggressive about it. You can send editors ideas for stories or completed pieces. Make contacts while you're still in school. You can always write a story on your own in your spare time for a local paper or a trade magazine.
>
> *Musical America*'s yearly issue has a complete list of various music trade publications. If you're a guitar player and have a new idea or approach that they haven't written about, send in a proposal. . . . You can start developing a name while you're still in school and make a few dollars as well.

"The best way to break into the field is to make a list of every person that's functioning in that field and go see them," advises Shirley Flemming.

> If you're good and persistent, something will eventually turn up. There are many more qualified people who can do music criticism than there are job openings. Someone once said, "The good music critics seldom retire and never die." There aren't very many jobs that open up. You might have to take another job while you are looking. . . . I had a period when

I first came to New York where I was hanging around between jobs. I was pretty close to getting into something else myself.

One person I know couldn't get a job, although he tried everything and was very well qualified. Finally, he went to work for a law firm for eight years and hated it. During that time, he kept going to school at night to improve his musical background. When a vacancy at *High Fidelity* magazine turned up, he got the job. People appreciated his single-minded determination and his extensive musical background. Finally, all his efforts paid off.

There is a very big element of luck in all of this. When I was knocking on doors, all of the critics I spoke to were sympathetic and open-minded. Many newspapers have cut down on their music coverage, and some papers in major cities don't even have a classical music critic. But one day they might decide to hire one and the right person knocking on the door at the right moment will get that job. . . . Critics, editors, and newspapers keep in touch through the Music Critics Association. They are a storehouse of information for anyone who is interested in music criticism.

Lifestyle

It is not as easy as one might think to go to a concert every single night, rush down to the newspaper, write and edit your review in an hour, and then feel fresh enough to go through the same thing the following night. Thomas Willis describes the working hours of a full-time critic as "awful." You are usually working well into the night by the time you finish rushing out your column. Even a part-time critic like Shirley Flemming works a full nine-to-five job as editor of *Musical America.* Then after what would be a normal working day for most people, she attends a concert, rushes down to the offices of the *New York Post,* and polishes off her review.

"There are times you get tired with the late nights," she says. "But you have to make a point of reminding yourself that you are writing for people to whom a concert is a special event, even though it's not a special event in my life."

There are, of course, some wonderful advantages in a music critic's life. One gets a chance to be an important factor in the artistic life of a community. If a critic's work becomes respected enough, that person's words will be quoted for many years to come. In addition, critics have an open door into the more glamourous and exciting parts of the music business. Tickets and recordings are free. Parties and openings are pleasant fringe benefits. Best of all, the critic who truly loves music gets to spend his life both listening to that music and bringing the musicians and works he really loves to public attention.

If you are one of the few lucky people who manage to become a full-time critic for a major publication, you might reach a salary level of $30-50,000 after many years. On the other hand, there are hundreds of good writers who get next to nothing for their pieces just to see them in print. Needless to say, these people have to find another way to put food on the table.

ROCK CRITICS

Rock critics face the same obstacles getting started and earning money as writers in the classical field. Like their colleagues in classical music, rock writers almost never limit themselves to criticism. They must be willing to do interviews, feature articles, and promotional writing. One can get started on the school or local paper very early in the game.

Since rock is not a particularly technical music, it is not usually considered necessary to have any musical background at all in order to write about it. In fact, some of the most successful rock writers have no musical grounding. This has led to a style of rock criticism that concentrates more on lyrics and current fashions than on the music itself. But the aspiring rock writer would do well to develop some practical knowledge of music as well as a thorough grounding in the earlier styles that have given shape to today's music. Without this kind of background, the rock critic has little to draw on beyond his own personal tastes.

Perhaps the fastest way to get your rock criticism in print is to line up an interview with a well-known star. If you can somehow speak to a Bob Dylan, Deborah Harry, or Stevie Wonder, you can be sure that somebody will include it in a publication. A number of writers have become rock gossip columnists and appear regularly in certain major newspapers. In the world of rock and pop, a performer's love life or rumors of a personnel change in a major group are of more interest to many readers than a perceptive discussion of music.

If you have a feel for popular music and a way with words, you have a real chance of getting published in your local or school newspaper. Try to find an interesting "angle." If you cannot line up an interview with a star, talk to the local concert promoter in your area about the problems of putting on concerts. Ask him which stars are easy to work with and why. When a name group is coming to your town, try to speak to the manager or one of the roadies and create an article from your conversations. If you have the ideas and the talent, you can start building your career as a rock writer while you are still in high school. Remember, you are also going to have to be aggressive and prepared to deal with rejection.

MUSIC PUBLICATIONS EDITING

Much of the writing one sees in music publications comes from outside freelance writers and is worked into shape by editors. Therefore, editors must have a good working knowledge of proofreading, copyediting, and layout. They also must possess a vital interest in literature, language, and the art of printing. On top of these skills, which good edi-tors in all fields need, a music publications editor also must have a thorough knowledge of the musical styles dealt with. William Anderson, editor of *Stereo Review*, advises young people who wish to get into music journalism "to consider language their first business (and) music their hobby." Still, a number of highly visible music editors did not major in English or journalism in college.

Roman Kozack, *Billboard*'s rock editor, started out by managing a local group in the town where he went to col-lege. Along with a partner, Kozack moved the band first to England and then to Rome, where they felt that the oppor-tunities would be better. "But the band collapsed," Kozack recalls, "just as most of these things do. After the band fell apart, I managed to get a job on the English language news-paper in Rome, where I wrote about sports and general news as well as music. In 1974, I became *Billboard*'s corre-spondent in Rome. And in 1976, I arrived at *Billboard*'s doorstep in New York. They hired me, first as a reporter and then as rock editor."

Roman Kozack likes his job. He especially enjoys writ-ing something good about a group that they can use to help their career. But he does not encourage young people to try to get involved in music journalism. "Nobody really makes a great deal of money in this field. The competition is great and there's no security. There are only a handful of publi-cations that pay anything and you really don't have that much of an effect on what's going on."

Shirley Flemming also does not foresee a great number of jobs opening up. But she feels that the rewards of a career in music journalism are many.

There's an opening here about once every ten years, so you have to be lucky in order to find a position. . . . The routines of copyediting and proofreading can get repetitive. But the mate-rials are always fresh because every subject and every approach is new. There are also marvelous things that open up to you on a job like this. I get to travel to various concerts and competitions all over the world, and it's great. That's why people hardly ever leave their positions.

Breaking Into The Field

The individual who is focusing on editing rather than writing should try to get a job with any publication that will hire him. A smaller company might provide the opportunity to acquaint yourself with more aspects of the business than would a major publication. People who wish to make careers in editing tend to move from job to job during their first few years in the field. As you master the requirements in any one company, you might do well to take a slightly better-paying offer that will provide you with new responsibilities. At the same time, you can pursue your interest in music by writing freelance articles. Then, when a rare opening as a music publications editor turns up, you might find that your extensive publishing background and your portfolio of music writings make you the most qualified person for the job.

PUBLIC RELATIONS WRITING

The success of any person or organization in the public eye depends on the image that is presented to the public through the media. This is no less true of musicians and singers than it is for politicians and big corporations. A public relations or press agent is hired by a client, often on a yearly basis, to keep the public aware of the activities of that client. If a singer is about to embark on a major tour, his or her press agent will inform the newspapers, magazines, and broadcast media of the tour through a press release.

A press release is a written statement that is somewhere in-between news and an advertisement. Editors get hundreds of press releases every week and must decide if there is enough news in a press release to merit taking up precious space in their publication. "I get twenty-five calls from press agents every day," says Shirley Flemming.

They all say, "I've got the greatest pianist you've ever heard. Why don't you put him on the cover?" Naturally, somebody in my position is bound to become resistant when you are constantly barraged with calls.

But press agents also perform an important function. Without them, I wouldn't know what important artists were doing. But I have to do a lot of filtering out and saying no because everybody wants to get their client into the magazine. There are a few really exceptional press agents and they do much more than simply let the press know about their artists' projects. They actually help set up the projects and make suggestions for programming. The really effective press agent functions like a manager in a way. If they are handling a music festival, they will try to get their clients into that festival. All editors tend to complain about press agents. But we do owe much of our information to their efforts.

Writing a Good Press Release

When Shirley Flemming discusses exceptional press agents, the name of Audrey Michaels quickly comes to mind. As someone who began her writing career as a journalist for the *New York Herald Tribune*, Audrey Michaels is dedicated to presenting only the facts in her press releases.

"It takes a great deal of skill to write a good and varied press release," she says. "I don't believe in adjectives and never use them in any of my materials. . . . When the history needs to be provided, I'll go out and dig it up because that's the way I was trained. Whenever I give seminars at colleges, I always try to encourage young people to use their imaginations. But I also stress the importance of checking and double-checking in order to get the facts straight. Any good press release should always answer the questions—who, what, why, when, and where."

Here is a recent press release written by Audrey Michaels. In spite of her dedication to facts, the materials are constructed to place the client in the best light. When a magazine editor like Shirley Flemming receives this press release, she might shorten it or take out facts that she does not consider important to her readers. On the other hand, Audrey Michaels complains that many newspaper reporters have gotten lazy and simply depend on using press releases almost word for word without first verifying their information.

NEWS

audrey michaels
Public Relations/Promotion • 122 East 76th Street • New York,
N. Y. 10021 • (212) 535-5533

FOR RELEASE: IMMEDIATE, PLEASE

PHILIPPE ENTREMONT APPOINTED
MUSIC DIRECTOR
NEW ORLEANS PHILHARMONIC
BEGINNING '81-82 SEASON

Philippe Entremont has been appointed Music Director and Conductor of the New Orleans Philharmonic Symphony beginning with the 1981–82 season, it was announced today by James J. Coleman, Sr., President of the New Orleans Philharmonic Symphony Society. The distinguished French conductor/pianist is the seventh Music Director of the 45-year-old orchestra, and in the 1981–82 season he will direct the orchestra in a minimum of ten of its sixteen subscription concert pairs.

In the 1980–81 season Philippe Entremont is Music Advisor for the orchestra. His new appointment as Music Director covers the 1981–82, '82–83, '83–84 seasons. Future plans include extended national tours and a European tour in the fall of 1982.

Mr. Entremont now is Music Director of orchestras on two continents, as he was appointed to this post with the Vienna Chamber Orchestra in 1976, and led the ensemble's second American tour in the 1979–80 season. He is part of the revival of the old tradition of major artists dividing their artistic activity between conducting and solo performance.

Previous conductors of the New Orleans Philharmonic have been: Leonard Slatkin, 1977–80; Werner Torkanowsky, 1963–77; James Yestadt (Associate Conductor), 1961–63; Alexander Hilsberg, 1952–60; Massimo Freccia, 1944–52; Olé Windingstad, 1939–44; and Arthur Zack, 1936–39.

Philippe Entremont will be heard as piano soloist with l'Orchestre du Capitole de Toulouse at the Kennedy Center Concert Hall in Washington, D.C. March 23, and at Carnegie Hall April 11, 1981.

The Role of a Press Agent

"The basic role of a press agent is to create an image of an individual performer or arts organization," says Audrey Michaels.

The image should be a viable one and present the facts the way they are. "Hype" is something awful that a lot of people go in for. But the lasting careers are built like a good house— with a solid basement, middle, and a solid roof. . . . I try to work only with those people that I really and truly believe in. I don't work with anyone who isn't first rate. So I feel free in suggesting features or television appearances for my clients.

Many people like to jump from press agent to press agent. But I really don't think that is a very good idea. You lose at least two years when you change press agents. I think it's far better to sit down and discuss your problems and see if they can be patched up. There are sometimes personality conflicts. You can't always get along with everybody. But I feel that two years is a very fair amount of time to give a new client. Then one knows if they have a good relationship and a productive relationship.

Clients must realize that they need good management, a record contract, and a good working relationship with their press agent. When a successful campaign is planned, it's always a team effort. With luck, it always works. But there is really no hard and fast formula for fame. . . . Like most of my colleagues, I work on a yearly retainer from my clients. But you can't really do very much in a year. That's why I always insist on a two-year commitment from all my clients.

Herb Karlitz has done public relations work for Melba Moore, Sammy Davis, Jr., and many other popular artists. Although most pop and rock acts have a shorter life-span than successful classical artists, the press agent for popular performers also tries to build lasting careers. Herb points to the placement of press releases and the setting up of interviews before an artist appears in a city as "the bread and butter of music business public relations." This requires a good working relationship with editors at the music trade magazines and contacts with journalists and other media people throughout the country.

Breaking into the Field

"People who want to break into music public relations have to read the trades (*Billboard, Cashbox, Record World* and *Radio and Records*) and know those trades," says Herb Karlitz.

You've got to keep up with what's going on in the business. What the new releases are. What the up and coming releases are. I know one person who took an album with a theme that he read about in the trades and wrote up an extensive public relations proposal. He sent it out to the label that released the album. They didn't use his ideas, but his energy and creativity were acknowledged. He had come up with a new approach for them, and they appreciated his effort. It's such a competitive business out there that anything you can do to get ahead is looked upon favorably.

Don't call up a record executive and say that you've got some great ideas for him. He probably won't even talk to you. But if you've taken the time to put together a treatment, someone will probably read it. . . . The conventional way of finding a job is knocking on all the doors of music business public relations firms. In recent times, that doesn't seem to be working out too well. Your chances are slim if you're doing the exact same thing that everyone else does.

Another way to go is to find an act or several acts and offer to work for them for free. Tell them that they only have to pay you if they make it and get that agreement in writing. A few years ago I needed to make $5000. So I went to the owners of a famous restaurant and said that I would promote their restaurant. I had done a good deal of public relations work, but I had never promoted a restaurant. I found myself in the kind of "Catch-22" situation that many people breaking into a field come up against. Nobody wants to hire you because you don't have any experience, and you can't get the experience unless somebody hires you. When the restaurant owners asked me if I ever had promoted a restaurant, I had to tell them no. But I guaranteed that I would get them more exposure than they ever saw. I said, "If you're not reasonably happy with my work, I'll give you your money back." That's how I got past their fears about my lack of experience.

Education and Training

Herb Karlitz feels that a big music public relations firm will only hire people who have a knowledge and understanding of the music business before they walk through the door. "That," he says, "is more important than having good public relations skills, although you need those too."

Audrey Michaels sees public relations in classical music as an important aspect of arts administration. "Get an MBA in the arts at a good school," she counsels. "Then get an internship working for a theatre or a private person. I really feel an MBA is essential today, plus the ability to write well. You should also not be above having office skills like typing and shorthand."

Many good public relations people have a background in journalism. Some major in that field in college, while others pick up skills working for newspapers. Sylvia Kraft, who manages promotion and press relations for Schirmer Music Publishers, feels that her newspaper background is a key in dealing successfully with editors.

> In every business, there's a certain formality about how to get things done in the right way. It's up to me to build up the contacts to call a guy on a paper or magazine and know what he is interested in. Someone has to be able to write things up in such a way that will excite editors to do a story. At the same time, I've got to get across the things that we want to emphasize. That's why my newspaper background comes in handy. I know what I used to stick into a wastepaper basket and what I actually used. I think that's a valuable experience, and I use it as a guide in communicating with the press now.

Like many other music-related careers, there are no strict guidelines for exactly what kind and how much education an individual needs. Each person finds his or her right path in a career like public relations. Still, Sylvia Kraft points out a number of attributes that would be helpful to any aspiring public relations person:

> You've got to have a certain amount of education and present yourself in a certain way. In what I do, I've got to write correctly, spell correctly, and pay close attention to facts. It certainly helps if you have a gift for dealing with people so

Sylvia Kraft, press and promotion manager at G. Schirmer, Inc. (gestu
ing in foreground) during an event she arranged celebrating critic Vir
Thomson's birthday. Thomson (seated) is visited by pianist Bobby
Short. (CHRIS TAYLOR)

that they want to deal with you on both sides (clients and media). You've got to be able to present yourself well and have a good sense of yourself.

Lifestyle and Money

Like most businesses that have a sales aspect to them, public relations can be a very lucrative field. A top independent press agent in pop or rock can earn a six-figure income. People who work for record companies or publishing houses will make substantially less. One must weigh the financial rewards against working with the type of music he or she is most comfortable with. Audrey Michaels has extensive training and a real love for classical music. Sylvia Kraft was a music major in college. She still does a good deal of playing and composing in her spare time. For these people, promoting classical music also means being close to something they deeply care about.

Some public relations people work for large companies and do some freelance work on the side. Others, like Sylvia Kraft, only publicize the clients who are signed to their companies. Audrey Michaels operates her very successful practice out of her home on New York's upper east side.

People rather like coming to where I live because they can sit, relax, and chat. And I like it because I can do as I please. If I want to work eight hours a day, I work eight hours. If I want to work fifteen hours a day, then that's what I do. But every day is a work day. You set certain disciplines for yourself. My secretary and the other people who work with me come in just as they would to a big office. We work very long and hard, but I feel the setting is more gracious.

For someone in public relations, it is particularly important to make people feel comfortable. Public relations is a very personal thing. It is really a peculiar kind of marriage. You have to like the person you work with and you also have to level with them. . . . This is not a good field for a person who is very tidy and can't do more than one thing at a time. To do well, you've got to know the business inside out. As in any business, you have to swallow a great deal. It isn't all peaches and cream, but if you really like what you're doing, then it's worth it.

Additional Sources for Information About Careers in Writing

MUSIC CRITICS ASSOCIATION OF AMERICA—6201 Tuckerman Lane, Rockville, Maryland 20852
"Promotes higher standards of music criticism in all media," and attempts to "increase general interest in music." It sponsors annual conventions and workshops and special projects for young critics.

PUBLIC RELATIONS SOCIETY OF AMERICA—INFORMATION CENTER—845 Third Avenue, New York, New York 10022
This is an excellent source of information and materials on publicity and public relations.

THE FREELANCE NETWORK—P.O. Box 149, Old Chelsea Station, New York, New York 10011
A good source of information and contacts for people pursuing freelance writing careers.

Publications

THE WRITER—(8 Arlington Street, Boston, Massachusetts 02166)
Provides excellent advice plus lists of markets (publications which might be potential buyers for your work). They also publish books about writing and marketing.

WRITER'S DIGEST—(9933 Alliance Road, Cincinnati, Ohio 9333)
Similar to *The Writer* but emphasis more on writing skills.

LESLY'S PUBLIC RELATIONS HANDBOOK—(Edited by Philip Lesly. Prentice Hall Inc., Englewood Cliffs, New Jersey: 1978)

HOW TO GET HAPPILY PUBLISHED—(By Judith Appelbaum and Nancy Evans. Harper and Row Publishers, New York: 1978)

CHAPTER 6

Careers in Radio

Of all the media, none lends itself so well to music as radio. In terms of hours and dollars, television is certainly bigger. The growth of videotapes, videodisks, and cable television is sure to have an impact on the future of radio. Still, it is likely that most Americans will spend some part of their day listening to either AM or FM radio. For one thing, many people enjoy listening to music while they are working or engaged in some other activity. Listening demands less of your total attention than looking. Most people can watch a great film twice or perhaps even five times, but they can listen to a favorite song hundreds of times. This is an important reason why radio is likely to retain its role as the leading medium for music.

Opportunities for work at radio stations are on the rise. Many new stations will be sprouting in the near future, and they will need qualified announcers, engineers, and sales personnel. Existing stations will be expanding or altering their formats, and they are always on the lookout for talented people with creative ideas.

FACT SHEET
CAREERS IN RADIO

Career	Opportunities for Employment	Education and Training	Skills and Personality Traits
ADVERTISING SALESPERSON (sells advertising time to sponsors, advertising agencies, and other buyers)	• All radio stations employ sales personnel • General managers of many radio stations come from the ranks of sales personnel	• A high school diploma is often sufficient although the broad background one receives from a liberal arts and/or a business course of study can be very helpful	• A thorough knowledge of the station's operations and programing • An understanding of one's target audience • A sensitivity to the needs of advertisers • Salesmanship and public relations skills

The Role Of Radio As Seen By the Pros

A wide range of issues in modern radio and career opportunities in this field will be discussed by the following professionals:

Matt Biberfeld—General manager and former program director of WNCN-FM, one of two full-time classical stations in New York.

Jim Cameron—Manager of Radio News for NBC Source Radio.

Mark Chernoff—Program director and morning personality of WDHA, a contemporary rock station in Dover, New Jersey.

Pete Fornatel—Midday host on New York's WNEW-FM, one of America's foremost progressive rock stations. Author of two books on radio.

Lifestyle	Earnings	Employment Outlook
• Regular daytime hours • Part of one's time is spent servicing established customers but some time must also be given to finding new customers	• Depending on how good one is and how hard one is willing to work, one can earn over $50,000 a year as a radio sales person	• Positions may not always be easy to locate but good sales people are always in demand in this industry

Bob Mahlman—Independent radio consultant for the RKO Network and others. Formerly a vice president at ABC Radio.

Walter Sabo—Vice President at NBC Radio.

Bob Vanderheyden—Program director of WCBS-FM, New York, a station closely identified with playing "oldies."

Education and Training

Most radio professionals agree that on-the-job training is the most sensible approach for a young person who seeks a career in radio. This means getting involved at your local radio station while you're still in school in any way you can. If you decide to go to college, pick a school with a good college radio station and work there. Except for Pete Fornatel, none of these radio professionals recommend that you major in broadcasting.

FACT SHEET
CAREERS IN RADIO

Career	Opportunities for Employment	Education and Training	Skills and Personality Traits
BROADCAST TECHNICIAN (Operate and maintain the electronic equipment used to record and transmit radio programs)	• All radio stations employ technicians • A small station might employ fewer than four while a large station might have more than ten	• The chief engineer must have a first class radio-telephone operators' license from the Federal Communications Commission • All other technicians need a third class license • In order to obtain these licenses one must pass a written exam • Technical schools and special college courses offer training for these tests • Hands-on experience at a college radio station provides a good basis for a technical career in radio	• Mechanical aptitude • Ability to work well as a key member of a team • Ability to handle full range of technical duties including promotion, maintenance, and repair responsibilities

Lifestyle	*Earnings*	*Employment Outlook*
• Sometimes have to work long hours under great pressures to meet broadcast deadlines	• Salary for a beginning technician is approx. $150 per week plus overtime • Salary for a chief engineer at a big station can be over $800 a week	• Beginners are likely to find job opportunities in smaller rather than larger markets • The number of positions might be reduced by future automation and technological advances

FACT SHEET
CAREERS IN RADIO

Career	Opportunities for Employment	Education and Training	Skills and Personality Traits
DISC JOCKEY (communicator, on-air personality)	Radio stations (Most disc jockeys start out in smaller markets)	• A broad base college education is recommended, at a school with a good college radio station • Some people also find employment after a short course in a private broadcasting school • Should have third class radio-telephone operators' license	• Good speaking and communication skills • Ability to relate to the audience you are trying to reach • A knowledge of the music one is playing and the lifestyle of one's audience
PROGRAM DIRECTOR (Administers station's programming policies)	• Every radio station employs a program director • Most program directors were disc jockeys first	• A college degree is usually desirable— courses in business and psychology can be helpful	• Knowledge of music • An understanding of the principles of business and advertising • An ability to supervise people • Accepting responsibility for what goes on the air • Ability to hire and fire personnel

Lifestyle	*Earnings*	*Employment Outlook*
• Most beginners must work late night shift • May occasionally have to work overtime per station requirements • Must read constantly to keep up to date on current events and musical trends	• Salary ranges from $8,000 a year for a beginner at a small station to $250,000 a year for a top DJ at a major A.M. station • The average salary is between $15,000 and $20,000 per year	• A good communicator with experience at a highly regarded college station should be able to find a job in a smaller market • There are expected to be more openings in the next few years but the competition is growing faster than the number of job openings
• Some program directors also work an on-air shift • Must be available in case of emergency • Must keep up to date with musical trends and needs of advertisers	• Moderate to good • An experienced program director at a major radio station can make between $45,000–$75,000 a year	• Good for experienced people with a solid track record in radio

"You should get from college those things that you can't get better someplace else," suggests Walter Sabo. "College can teach you English literature, sociology, foreign languages, and philosophy better than the real world."

"Don't major in broadcasting," Jim Cameron states emphatically.

> Broadcasting majors are a waste. I've never hired one of them. You don't need to sit in a classroom and hear someone lecture you on how to read a meter or clean a record. . . . I recommend that you major in something that's going to help you adjust to the changing times and deal with the world. Major in psychology, journalism, or sociology. Work at the college radio station. Those are the best places to gain experience. You can work in a variety of positions and you can make mistakes. Then when you graduate, you can work your way through the ranks—from smaller to larger markets.
>
> When you're in college, try to get a credit-bearing internship where you can go to work as an apprentice. But you've got to sell yourself. You will only succeed if you have a positive mental attitude. If you hustle, you can do well. If you don't hustle, nobody is going to give you anything on a silver platter.

Bob Vanderheyden feels that hands-on experience is the key to a successful radio career. As the only one of these successful professionals who did not attend college, it is not surprising that he does not place much weight on formal education. "My advice to a young person is to get out of high school and find a job. If you can somehow mix the practical experience with schooling, that's fine. But don't expect to finish four or ten years of college and just walk into a job. Many students graduate college, can't find jobs, and get disillusioned."

Pete Fornatel has a somewhat different point of view. He advocates attending a college with a strong radio station and majoring in broadcasting. "I majored in communications and chose other courses to help broaden my perspective. . . . There's no question in my mind that most future broadcasting talent will come from the ranks of college media. The current rule seems to be that a couple of years at a modern, well-run college station is better than working your way up from smaller to larger markets. I'm proof of that. I went right from college to a job on New York radio."

Broadcast Schools

The Yellow Pages in any big city will contain a number of broadcasting schools. These places offer training programs that can range from six weeks to a year. Although a number of professionals take a dim view of such schools, others feel that some of them are well worth looking into. Apparently, there is no organization that supervises and rates schools of broadcasting. Some of these places are only interested in a person's money. But others do offer good training programs and placement assistance. How does one find out which schools are worthwhile?

"Get off your butt and reach exactly seven inches to the telephone," counsels Bob Mahlman. "That's sometimes tough for a young person to do, but that's what you need to do. . . . Find out from potential employers how they feel about particular schools. Call up the program director of a radio station and ask him. When you check out a school, ask them: How much money will it cost? What credentials do they have? What kind of state licensing do they have? Where are their former graduates now working? Speak to some current students at the school. Find out every aspect about that school before you spend your money."

Whether or not a person majors in broadcasting, the consensus seems to be that a college education plus experience at a college radio station is more useful than a certificate from a broadcasting school. "Some of those schools will accept people they shouldn't take," says Mark Chernoff. "Radio is an entertainment field and some people will do anything to get into it. Unfortunately, some schools prey on this. Others are better. The best sources of information about schools are people at a radio station. You might also check the Department of Consumer Affairs to see if there are any claims against a school."

Breaking into the Field

Probably the most direct way to break into the radio business is to try to get a job at your local radio station—any kind of job. If there are no jobs available at that time, you might even offer your services for nothing.

"If you want to get started," counsels Bob Vanderheyden, "hang around the local radio station. I started hanging around when I was in high school. Eventually, I had coffee with the chief engineer. Later, I got to know the general manager, and eventually he let me go on the air."

If you are interested in becoming a disc jockey or announcer, you can practice your skills in your own room with almost any kind of a tape recorder. "You need a good speaking voice and you can get a sense of delivery on your own," advises Matt Biberfeld.

But you have to be very self-critical and compare your delivery to what you are hearing on the radio. Almost anyone can be good for an hour. But people on the air have to be good four hours a day, six days a week, month after month. They have to keep sounding fresh, as though sitting in that little windowless room is the most exciting thing they can be doing. That's a practiced trick that is akin to being an actor.

There is also a great deal of technical stuff involved in radio which is invisible to the listeners at home. Announcers often have to cue records up, run their own board, get together

Matt Biberfeld (left) of radio station WNCN interviews violinist Isaac Stern on his weekly show "Metropolitan Arts." (VALLÉE)

newscasts, and make transmitter readings. These skills are all necessary for modern radio operation. Many smaller stations don't even have engineers. Announcers do the whole thing.

Assume a person has acquired the basic skills. How does he or she get that first job? "There are three steps to getting a job in radio," says Bob Vanderheyden. "The first is who you know. The second is timing. And the third is ability. In that order. You will get the job on who you know and timing. But you will keep the job on ability. . . . Radio isn't the glamour business it once was. It's a business business, and you had better know what you're doing."

"Learn a lot of different skills," suggests Jim Cameron.

Get a broad base and try to do as many things as possible. When you're in college you don't really know what you are going to wind up doing. I thought I would be a DJ, but now I'm doing news. There are very few jobs in radio where a person does only one thing. When I was working on WCOZ in Boston, I was the Director of Public Affairs. I was also a weekend DJ and I also wrote public service announcements. The more things you can do, the more valuable you are going to be to your potential employer.

If you walk in and apply for a job as a DJ and you can also say: "Here are some examples of things I've produced. I can do interviews. I can do sock hops and television appearances. I have a talent for art and I can help design the station's artwork." Any of these skills is going to help you get the job. So the idea is: *Get as broad an education as you can, and learn as much about the business as you can.* You've got to be hungry and you've got to be learning all the time.

"Don't come to me with a resume," cautions Walter Sabo.

Come to me with an idea. Show me what you can do. Call me up and say, "I have an idea. I can show you how to do something better than you're doing it." No good executive will turn down the opportunity to hear a good idea. If somebody calls me up and says, "I really want to come and work for you. Would you talk to me?" The answer is almost always yes. I get tons of resumes, but very few of them come with a letter that says, "I want to see you. . . ." I find mass mailings very insulting. I'm not going to send back a personal letter to a xeroxed resume. So the key is: Come in with a written idea and show me how this business can be made better. . . . You may not get the job, but at least you'll get in the door.

There are thousands of people out there who want to work in radio. Maybe ten of them are worth anything. Those are the ones we'll grab. To work at one of our stations in a major market, you'd better have a pretty solid background. We're not in the big markets to teach. We do have some internship programs in conjunction with colleges. When we have the money, we also try to provide summer jobs. Any young person who would rather spend his summer at a radio station instead of at the beach is someone we have to look at pretty seriously. I always lined up my summer jobs before Christmas. You can try to contact the station (NBC) in January.... The key is wanting to be good and being in love with the work. If you are really in love with broadcasting, you'll probably be good.

DJ'S, COMMUNICATORS, AND ON-AIR PERSONALITIES

Disc jockeys are the up-front people in the radio business. Theirs are the voices that fill the airways. Some of them have become stars in their own right. A few have even been credited with launching musical trends. Alan Freed, for example, is often cited as an important figure in popularizing rock 'n' roll among white teenagers in the 50's. But the role of the DJ has changed significantly over the years. The changes were, in great part, due to the payola scandal which came to a head in 1960.

Record companies depend on radio play as an important component in the creation of a hit record. When a record promotion man hands a new record to a DJ and asks him to play it, he recognizes that his record might be only one of a hundred new releases that the DJ receives that week. If the promo man presents the record to the DJ over a good meal in a fancy restaurant and then picks up the tab, we can consider that as part of the normal wining and dining that goes on in many businesses. But what if the record company is providing the DJ with expensive gifts or large amounts of cash in exchange for special considerations? The extent of such pay-for-play practices were not clearly established by the payola hearings of 1959–60. But there was no doubt that a number of important DJ's were accepting favors in return for giving certain records priority treatment.

As a response to the payola hearings, radio stations instituted play-lists and formats, so that DJ's no longer had control over what records they played. Although many stations have had numerous programming changes over the years, DJ's have never regained the power they once had. But the people who communicate over the air are still the hub of the radio business. No matter what records they are or are not playing, radio stations cannot succeed if the public does not respond to the person whose voice is coming into their homes, offices, and cars.

"DJ's prefer to be called communicators or personalities, and that's really what they are," explains Bob Mahlman.

> Radio is one to one. It's intimate. There's nothing you do in your life, except sleep, that you can't do and listen to a radio. The good communicators know how to get across to their audiences. Certain personalities can project one to one. The voice isn't really that big of a deal. A good communicator should be comfortable rapping about anything.
>
> Good communicators are well-rounded people who spend time reading, watching, and observing. They are people who see meaningful things in life and are able to talk about them. You have to read newspapers and stay on top of things that are occurring . . . and work these things in for the people the station is trying to reach. You'd better know your audience and how they live. You don't have to be twenty in order to communicate to twenty-year olds, but you'd better know all about them. . . . The successful people I know are not ad-libbers. They prepare a full day in advance. . . .
>
> The effective communicator doesn't just come on the air and say, "Hello, this is good old Bob." It's more like; "Good morning. I don't care what you're doing, but let's talk a little bit. Here's a piece of music. Here's what's going on in the

world. . . ." Most of the successful stations in this country re-
volve around the morning person. Becoming a good communicator is a study. It's not an accident. It's a lot more than saying,
"Hey, I've got a good voice. I can talk." The best people in
the profession look at it as a twenty-four hour business that
you have to study. It takes a lot of effort, preparation, and
hard work.

Many talented communicators move into programming
or other management positions. Some, like Jim Cameron,
feel that rigid play-lists have taken much of the creativity
out of being a DJ. "Even though the program director decides which records are played," he points out, "the DJ is
often the one to get fired if the station's ratings go down.
An incredible amount of pressure can be brought to bear
on a DJ if an advertiser doesn't like something he says on
the air. Advertisers have millions of dollars to spend on ads,
and they can really put the screws to you. God grant a DJ
the serenity to deal with a general manager who says,
'You've cost me a quarter of a million dollars of business.
You're fired.' Things like that happen all the time."

Pete Fornatel is that rare personality who works at a station where he can select records that he likes. Still, he realizes that if his station's ratings go down, things can change
in a hurry. "I'm spoiled because I've always had a say in
what I'm doing. . . . Many DJ's I know have left the business because of the lack of freedom that has now become
the rule. . . . I would probably consider an alternate career
rather than submit to that kind of mentality. And I know
that's a real possibility."

Some radio personalities are not particularly concerned
with the kind of music they play. In fact, there are some
people in the business who don't even particularly like
music. "I didn't get into radio because I love music,"
Walter Sabo admits candidly. "I got into radio because I
wanted to be on the air. In fact, I considered the records an

intrusion because it meant that there was less time for me to be on the air. Now, more than ever, you don't need a particularly good feel for music to be an effective personality because very few DJ's pick their own records."

Formats and Ratings

Stations program certain kinds of music in order to achieve the highest possible ratings in a particular market. Since radio is financed by the dollars that advertisers spend to buy time on the air, program directors must know who their audience is. Advertisers want to know the demographics of a station's audience. How old are the listeners? How much money do they make? What kinds of products do they buy? These are the kinds of facts that advertisers want to know before they decide how much money they are going to spend on which stations and at what time of the day.

Today's radio stations are out to attract very specific segments of the population. Unlike some stations in the past which programmed different kinds of music at different times of the day in order to attract a variety of listeners, today's radio stations are characterized by programming which appeals to a particular type of listener. This trend has come to be called *narrow*casting as opposed to *broad*casting. Here are a number of programming formats that are usually found in every major market: AOR (Album oriented rock); Top 40; MOR (Middle of the Road); Beautiful Music; Black Music; Ethnic Music; Country Music; Classical Music; Jazz; Talk Radio; All-News Radio.

If a particular format is not attracting a large enough percentage of the audience, it will often be changed in a hurry. A survey in 1980 indicated that if WLIB—an FM jazz station in New York—switched its format to country music, a substantially larger number of listeners would tune that station in. In spite of the protests of angry jazz fans, the station adopted a country music format. Most of the DJ's stayed on with the station, even though they had become identified with a completely different kind of music.

Walter Sabo describes the way NBC surveys its audiences: "Our researchers call a certain number of homes and ask people what they like and how they feel about what we are playing. We put that information into a computer which selects and balances the music we play . . . so that the listener can listen for a long time."

Program Director Bob Vanderheyden is among those radio executives who are skeptical about surveys and ratings.

> The various rating companies will tell you that radio is a science. But I don't believe that. . . . I feel that most of the surveys and ratings that are taken are not accurate. They tend to reflect the method of that particular rating company rather than what the public wants. Instead of reflecting the thinking of the public, ratings tend to affect that thinking. Of course, many stations abide by ratings because of the financial and sales pressures which are brought to bear.
>
> When radio started out, the thing was to put on a good program and then sell it. Then we went through a period where the sales department got a hold on the radio stations and they were trying to sell something they didn't have. Instead of paying attention to programming, they broke it down into figures. You can't really do that in radio because you are dealing with human nature, moods, and fads. How can you rate that stuff? Personally, I don't react to surveys, although I do look at ongoing trends.

No matter how an individual executive might feel, most stations live and die by ratings. This trend has also affected the way musicians craft their sound and select material for an album. More than ever, music business and radio people are not so much concerned with whether a record is good. The more important questions often are: What kind of a song is it, and what kind of radio format will it fit into? This way of thinking has placed a radio station's program director in a position of great importance.

PROGRAM DIRECTOR

Like most program managers, Mark Chernoff began his career as a DJ. His bosses at station WDHA in Dover, New Jersey, took note of his MBA education, and moved him into a mangement position within two years. Although he still works the station's morning shift as a DJ, Mark's responsibilities have become more complex.

> I spend a good deal of time reading trade publications like *Billboard, Radio and Records* and *Record World.* I call up record stores in this area to see which records are moving. I also have to use my own ear for music to decide if a certain record fits into the structure I'm looking for. We play a certain number of oldies and I must make sure that these also fit our format. My responsibilities also include a lot of day-to-day things. I have to make sure that everybody is here for their shifts. I go over air-checks with people to see what their good and bad points are. I work with the news department to see that we're running the kind of news that's appropriate.
>
> Basically, I make sure that everything comes together. I write some of our promotions, and I try to make them effective. Right now, we're promoting a WDHA Discount Card that we hope to run forever. I meet with the general manager and work with him on promotions and play-lists. I also hire and train the new people who come to work at the station. On top of all this, I have to listen to a lot of records. And, of course, I have to make sure that we don't get into a situation where it's Saturday night and someone says: "Hey, there's no DJ here. . . ."

Program director and DJ Mark Chernoff on the air at WDHA.

Lifestyle and Money

"Radio is a tough business," says Matt Biberfeld.

The perception that radio is a big money business is false. The average salary for a DJ is probably no more than around $15,000 a year. Of course, the top DJ's in a market like New York can make much more. The big money in this business is in sales.... Also, the person who plans to make a career as a violinist or a singer and thinks he can go into radio as a second choice has the wrong attitude. Many people who go into radio have that as their primary career goal. They are going to work harder and cheaper than someone who is doing it because he can't do the thing he really wants to do....

Because radio is a part of show business, people think of it as a glamourous profession. But it turns out to be a lot of hard

221

work with limited chances for success. . . . In general, radio is a
dog-eat-dog business with a lot of backbiting, a lot of competition, and limited salaries.

In spite of the drawbacks and pitfalls, the people who
work in radio seem to love what they are doing. "I
wouldn't want to work in any other field," says Bob Vanderheyden. Jim Cameron is even more enthusiastic. "If
they weren't paying me to do my job," he confesses, "I
would do it for free." Pete Fornatel has a similar attitude:
"What my bosses don't know and what I never want them
to find out is that I was doing the very same thing they are
paying me nicely to do here for nothing (in college) for six
years of my life. It's nice to be able to have made that transition and to make a living at something you really care
about."

Although Pete only works five four-hour shifts on the
radio, his job requires many hours of preparation. Still, he
finds as he has gotten older, his priorities have changed.

> I've been unusually fortunate. I came to this job from school
> teaching, and the hours are even better here because I work the
> 10-2 P.M. shift. I've been at WNEW for twelve years and they
> have been years of tremendous change. When I got here, I was
> single and had few responsibilities and roots. Now, twelve
> years later, I'm married with three sons and a home in the sub-
> urbs. When I got here . . . I used to go to every concert and
> every opening. Now, given the choice between staying in town
> to see a concert or going home and spending time with my
> kids, I opt for the latter.
>
> The younger people who work at the station like to go to all
> of the shows. But these days, I'd rather take the early train
> home. Still, you must stay aware of the industry in which you
> work. I still read the trade papers and talk to people in the in-
> dustry to keep abreast of what's going on.

Bob Mahlman feels that a really effective radio personality must have a total commitment to communicating with his or her audience.

Good radio communication involves every experience that a person has. The effective communicator must be able to study the life experiences of others within certain age brackets. If he is good, he can move up quickly. A person working his first job at a small station might only make $10–12,000 a year. A top morning personality in a major market can make up to $250,-000 a year. There are also many opportunities for additional work. DJ's can get a percentage of what is sold on their program. They can do concert work or personality hosting. Eventually, many of them will become program directors.

For the first time, program directors are making as much money as sales directors. Years ago, you could get a program director for almost nothing. But now, stations are beginning to understand that the programming makes the audience and the sales will follow. There still aren't many program directors making $100,000 a year. But the good ones at major stations are making between $45–70,000.

WOMEN AND MINORITIES IN RADIO

There is probably less discrimination based on sex and race in radio than in most other industries. For one thing, the Federal Communications Commission (FCC) demands that radio stations offer equal opportunities for qualified individuals. In addition, the stations must employ a similar percentage of people as they are represented in the general population. If, for example, blacks constitute 20 percent of a community's population, a radio station in that market must employ blacks as 20 percent of its total staff.

Women have made tremendous inroads into radio, particularly in the area of sales. "My entire sales staff is women," says Matt Biberfeld. "My business manager is a woman and so is my general manager. Up until the 60's, radio was mostly a male business, probably because of the notion that women could not handle technical equipment. But now that those stereotypes have broken down, there are more women in all areas of radio." Bob Mahlman also finds that women are becoming a dominant force in radio. "Because of the FCC rules, women are sought after. At the RKO Network, the news director and the program director are both women, as well as the entire production staff of non-news programming. There are also three or four women newspeople.

Although the FCC regulations cover ethnic minorities as well as women, there are a number of considerations that come into play. A station that is programming for a black audience will usually have all black DJ's. But classical stations, on the other hand, may employ only white people as on-air personalities. "Classical music tends to come out of the European heritage," Matt Biberfeld points out. "So it is sometimes difficult to find third-world announcers who fit the image of the station. But in general, I don't see any limitation because of sex or race. . . . The opportunities for any individual in radio are only limited by that individual's imagination."

Additional Sources for Information About Careers in Radio

FEDERAL COMMUNICATIONS COMMISSION—Washington, D.C. 20554

NATIONAL ASSOCIATION OF BROADCASTING— 1771 N. W. Street, Washington, D.C. 20036

CORPORATION FOR PUBLIC BROADCASTING—1111 16th Street N.W. Washington, D.C. 20036

RADIO ADVERTISING BUREAU—485 Lexington Avenue, New York, New York 10017

Publications

BROADCAST ENGINEERING—1014 Wyandotte, Kansas City, Missouri 64105

BROADCASTING—1736 DeSales Street N.W., Washington, D.C. 20036

TELEVISION/RADIO AGE—1270 Avenue of the Americas, New York, New York 10020

RADIO AND RECORDS—1930 Century Park West, Los Angeles, California 90067

ENCYCLOPEDIA OF RADIO & T.V. BROADCASTING—Milwaukee, Cathedral Square: 1970.

CHAPTER 7

Technical and Scientific Careers in Music

RECORDING ENGINEER

"The engineer's most important role is to create an environment in the recording studio so that people can make music," says Brad Leigh. After five years of moving up through the ranks, Brad has built a reputation as one of New York's most promising young engineers. He has worked on recording sessions for Paul Simon, Billy Joel, and other top stars. Like all successful engineers, Brad has mechanical ability, a good technical knowledge of all the equipment used in recording studios, an ear for music, and an ability to deal with people.

Brad Leigh at the controls as a recording engineer.

Education and Training

Many engineers take a six-month course and then try to get
a "goffer" job at any recording studio that will take them
on. There are also an increasing number of colleges offering degree programs in the art and science of recording engineering. But, as Brad Leigh points out, "Most of these
college graduates will have to start at the bottom of the lad-

FACT SHEET
TECHNICAL AND SCIENTIFIC CAREERS

Career	Opportunities for Employment	Education and Training	Skills and Personality Traits
RECORDING ENGINEER (Mixer)	• Recording studios • Live concerts	• College plus recording studio experience • Or short course (approx. 6 months) plus recording studio experience	• Mechanical aptitude • Technical knowledge of recording equipment • Knowledge of music • Ability to work under pressure and to please clients
INSTRUMENT BUILDER AND REPAIR PERSON	• Large companies • Small stores • Your own business	• College courses in instrument technology (6 months to 2 years) helpful • Courses in music and woodworking also helpful • Apprenticeship with master craftsman (4–5 years of on-the-job training) necessary	• Mechanical aptitude • Manual dexterity • Knowledge of instrument(s) you are working on • Dedication to your work • Desire to serve clients • Good hearing
ACOUSTICIAN	• Corporations involved with noise control • Architectural and engineering companies • Acoustical consulting firms	• College degree in architecture, engineering, or physics desirable	• Knowledge of architecture and engineering • Knowledge of music and other performing arts

Lifestyle	Earnings	Employment Outlook
• Night and weekend work • Long and irregular hours • Most top engineers work freelance	• Minimum wage for assistants • Top engineers can make from $50,000 to $100,000	• Competitive at the present time • Fewer openings anticipated in the next few years
• Long hours for successful people with their own businesses • Pensions and company benefits for those working with big companies • Work relatively safe; may suffer small cuts and bruises when making repairs	• Beginning rate for helpers $3 to $5 per hour • Experienced workers with companies $5–$10 per hour • Experienced craftsmen with their own business can earn up to $25,000	• Hard to obtain first position; best opportunities for beginners are with dealerships and large repair shops
• Regular hours • Some travel	• Salary range approx. $15,000 to $40,000	• Opportunities should increase in this growing new field • Somewhat tied to the number of new concert facilities being constructed

der anyway." As the technology of recording becomes more advanced, college degrees may become more prevalent. But most of the top engineers in the business today do not have any formal college training in engineering.

If you plan to go to college and have an interest in engineering, you might benefit from courses in music and electronics. If you can take an elective or two in the theory and practice of engineering recording sessions, by all means do so. But remember, no matter how extensive your knowledge or educational background, your first engineering job will consist mostly of sweeping floors, going for coffee, and watching more experienced people at work.

Breaking In

Shortly after high school graduation, Brad took a six-month course at a technical school. A friend of his knew the owner of a small New York recording studio called Chelsea Sound. After a brief interview, Brad was hired as an assistant. "Before that, I went around to every studio in the city with my resume offering to do anything," Brad remembers. "But Chelsea was a good place for me to start. Because it was a small studio, I got a chance to do a variety of things right away. I got to assist on sessions and talk to clients on the telephone. After a few months, I had a good picture of the entire operation."

Brad had always been good at fixing electronic equipment. He quickly realized that this ability would make him an invaluable asset to a studio. If a piece of equipment breaks down in the middle of a recording session, a person who can quickly restore that equipment to working order is extremely valuable. Within a few short months, Brad became the most skilled maintenance person on the staff. Because he could provide such a needed service, his salary increased. Also, the owner of the studio permitted him to experiment with the recording equipment during off hours. Brad established his reputation very quickly. He was soon hired to do maintenance engineering at the much larger A&R Studios. Here he got an opportunity to work with some of the best producers, engineers, and recording artists in the business. Today he engineers many sessions for Phil Ramone, a record producer who handles Paul Simon, Billy Joel, and many others. Brad also does a good deal of freelance engineering .

Brad feels that his rapid development was a result of natural talent and getting an opportunity to work in a small studio. He advises young people who wish to break in to take any kind of job in any studio that will have them. Here is his description of how an assistant works his or her way up the ladder at a large studio.

You start out sweeping floors and running messages. If they like you, you get to work in the library for six months to a year storing tapes. Then, you begin making tape copies. It's a very long and involved process before you get to actually assist on a recording session.

I feel that people who start at the bottom and work their way up really get a much better understanding of what they're doing. An assistant engineer sets up a session. He positions all of the microphones, instruments, and amplifiers in the room and makes sure that everything is working. He also must make sure that there is enough tape for the session and keep a record of the takes of all the songs. . . . The assistant engineer is responsible for all the equipment that is needed at the session. Very often, the assistant will run the tape machine.

The way an assistant works determines the pace of a session. If he doesn't have all of the equipment set up on time, the session will be delayed. And if a problem comes up, the assistant's ability to straighten it out quickly can help keep the session moving at a good pace.

Some people never get beyond being good assistant engineers. Assistants don't have to hear especially well or know how to select the right equipment for a particular session. An assistant might know how to set up a microphone, but that doesn't mean he necessarily knows how to choose one.

Lifestyle

A recording engineer must be prepared to work long and varied hours. A commercial might be booked at nine in the morning, while a vocal session for an album may last well beyond midnight. "No matter how successful you become," Brad notes, "you can never really pick the hours you want to work. If you take on a project, you have to accept complete responsibility for working on it whenever you're called. Maybe after you've finished a major project, you can take a little time off if you work freelance. But while you're working, there is no such thing as regular hours."

An important part of the lifestyle of an engineer is working under pressure with different people. You might get involved in a session with a producer whom you cannot stand. But as a professional, it is your responsibility not to let that affect your work. This kind of situation comes up quite often with engineers who work on the staff of recording studios. They simply must be able to work with anyone who is paying for the time.

"You have to try and please everybody," Brad advises. "particularly at the beginning of your career. You can't show a bad attitude or you won't develop any new clients. I remember somebody I met my first day at Chelsea told me that he wouldn't give me a hard time because in a year, I could be president of a record company. This business is just too small to have problems with too many people. You have to please clients or you're not going to get more work. It's as simple as that."

Financial Considerations

An assistant engineer at a major studio usually makes the minimum wage. A top freelance engineer gets a high hourly fee and can sometimes make deals for royalty percentages. Brad Leigh estimates that the top engineers make between fifty and one hundred thousand dollars a year. "But no matter how good the money eventually gets," he adds, "engineering still is an unstable business. If you accept a four month project from a record company and it falls through, you can suddenly find yourself with no work. I started out expecting to work my way into a stable financial situation. But if you consider all of the time you put in, the ridiculous hours, and the sacrifices in your personal life, the money is not as terrific as you hope it will be."

INSTRUMENT BUILDING AND REPAIR

There are two ways to look at careers in instrument building and repair. On one level, they are good industrial jobs for people who wish to combine an interest in music with mechanical ability. On another level, the building and repairing of instruments is a fine craft for a person of rare talent and dedication.

Roger Sadowsky is certainly in the second category of instrument craftspersons. When he gave up his doctoral fellowship in psycho-biology to apprentice with a guitar maker, his family was more than a little concerned. But Roger had become obsessed with building fine guitars.

> Nobody in my family was a craftsman. They were all professional people. I was a folk guitar player, and I got obsessed with how guitars were made. I started reading catalogues and memorizing all of the specifications. . . . I realized halfway

Guitar-builder Roger Sadowsky considers his work a labor of love.

through my doctoral studies that this was the work for me. I knew from the kind of surgery I was doing in graduate school that I had the manual dexterity to be a craftsman.

Education and Training

An increasing number of schools are offering courses in instrument building and repair. But Roger Sadowsky and many of his colleagues believe that the old-fashioned way of apprenticing with a master craftsman is the best form of training. Most people who seek these apprenticeships have some knowledge of the instrument(s) they wish to work on and a good mechanical aptitude.

"It's not always that easy to become an apprentice with the type of person who can really teach you something," Roger observes.

It takes quite a bit of time to train somebody so that they can become productive. I've trained quite a few apprentices over the last few years and it usually takes them six months to a year to justify a minimum wage salary. The single most important factor in the success or failure rate of my apprentices is their motivation. When I hire somebody, it has nothing to do with demonstrating any particular manual dexterity or great knowledge of guitars. I look for somebody who wants to work on guitars more than anything else.

It takes a long time to become really good at what you're doing. I've been doing this for ten years and I'm just really coming into my prime. I would say that after two years of being an apprentice, a talented and dedicated person would need about ten years of constant work to put it all together.

Lifestyle and Money

Roger Sadowsky's workshop is on a busy Manhattan street corner. He lives in a small apartment that is attached to the space in which he works. Although he maintains office hours between 10 A.M. and 4 P.M., he works between fifty and seventy hours a week.

It's not uncommon for me to work seven days a week . . . but as hard as I work and as good as I am at what I do, I still find it difficult to make a moderate living. I'm still single and I really don't need that much. But I couldn't support a wife and kids on what I make.

This is not a field that you get into for the money. You only get involved in this because you love the work. If you're really good and bust your butt for ten years building a reputation, you can make a moderate living. But you'll never get rich.

I've had some offers from big companies to design and supervise the production of guitars for them. If I got involved in something like that, I could make more money and work fewer hours . . . but I think I'd get bored doing that. I prefer doing exactly what I want. After all, I'm in this for love, not money.

After spending years working on the guitars of some of New York's top studio players, Roger is becoming more involved in building his own electric guitars which he calls *Dr. Frets*. He feels that successful craftsmen do not impose their own preferences on the musicians they serve. Instead, they pride themselves on tailoring their work to the needs and preferences of the individual player.

"I try to create for myself a sense of how the musician experiences his guitar and work from there. . . . I've come to realize that there is no (special) value in guitars. A guitar is just a hunk of wood with some metal accessories. The real value of what I do comes from serving the person who owns the guitar. . . . That's where the interpersonal communication comes in. The guitar itself is just the medium."

ACOUSTICIAN

There is a new world of opportunities in the field of acoustics for people with a desire to work in a growing area of science and engineering. Acoustical engineers are involved with noise control in offices, schools, and hospitals. When architects design buildings, they are concerned with controlling and containing sound. Acoustical engineers are specialists who deal with the sound of particular structures or types of equipment.

The importance of acousticians in the designing of concert halls and other performance facilities cannot be overestimated. Sound is not just another issue in the creation of such buildings. It is the major issue.

As one of the important pioneers in the field of concert hall acoustics, Christopher Jaffe feels that many concert facilities have not been properly engineered:

Sound is still a mystery to many concert hall owners and operators. They plan everything very carefully: The sets, lighting, great musical productions, and wonderful costumes. Then when it's all finished, they put a microphone on the stage and hope for the best. . . . People who present rock concerts don't seem to give a great deal of thought to what they are doing when they present their attractions. They just turn the sound up louder and louder, and that reduces the musical quality of the performance. That's why the sound of a record is often so much better than that of a live performance.

Christopher Jaffe is quick to point out that there is no right acoustical structure for a facility.

Acoustics must be thought of in relation to a particular kind of music. The requirements are different for symphony orchestras, chamber music groups, and rock bands. Some new halls are built along the lines of an older hall that accommodates symphony orchestras when the new hall will probably be housing mostly popular concerts. . . . There are various baffles that can be brought in to tighten the sound. But no one hall can be acoustically perfect for every situation.

Education and Training

Being an acoustician is a relatively new profession. People in the field come from a variety of backgrounds. But anyone planning to make a career in this growing area should get a college degree in engineering or architecture. A background in music is a big plus for those who plan to specialize in the development of facilities and equipment for the performing arts.

The National Council of Acoustical Consultants and the Acoustical Society of America can provide further information about the growing number of colleges and universities offering courses in this field.

The first "surround" auditorium in America is Boettcher Hall in Denver, Colorado, designed by Christopher Jaffe. (COURTESY OF AUDREY MICHAELS)

Lifestyle and Money

Although companies that are concerned about noise control employ acoustical engineers, most acousticians are self-employed consultants or employees of consulting firms. Although Christopher Jaffe has devoted much of his energies to designing many of the great indoor and outdoor concert facilities in America, he also gets involved with non-musical acoustical facilities such as offices and schools.

The present salary range for acoustical consultants is about $15,000 for a recent college graduate to approximately $35-40,000 for an experienced consultant with extensive experience.

Outlook

Although the demand for acousticians is tied to the number of buildings and performing arts facilities being constructed, there is likely to be an increasing need for specialists in this area. It is still a field in which a lot of new ground remains to be broken. If you want to enter a profession that requires an interest in both science and music, the field of acoustics might be something worth looking into.

Additional Sources for Information About Technical and Scientific Careers in Music

PIANO TECHNICAN GUILD—113 Dexter Avenue North, Seattle, Washington 98109
    Also publishes *Piano Technicans Journal.*

AUDIO-ENGINEERING SOCIETY—60 E. 42nd Street, New York, New York 10017

ELECTRONIC INDUSTRY ASSOCIATION—2000 I. Street N.W., Washington D.C. 20006

GUITAR AND ACCESSORY MANUFACTURE ASSOCIATION OF AMERICA—4800 Chicago Beach Drive, Chicago, Illinois 60615

NATIONAL ASSOCIATION OF BAND INSTRUMENT MANUFACTURERS—1500 New Highway, Farmingdale, New York 11735

ACOUSTICAL SOCIETY OF AMERICA—335 E. 45th Street, New York, New York 10017

NATIONAL COUNCIL OF ACOUSTICAL CONSULTANTS—P.O. Box 359, 66 Morris Avenue, Springfield, New Jersey 07081

CHAPTER 8

Part-time Opportunities for Young People

Here are ten suggestions for paying jobs in music and music related fields that you can pursue while you are still in school:

1. *MUSICIAN/SINGER*—Join an existing local band or put one together. Advertise in local papers and on the bulletin board of your local music store.

2. *MUSIC TEACHER*—If you are skilled on an instrument, you might be able to get a job teaching beginners at your local music store. Or you can go into business yourself by offering your services to friends and relatives at a

reasonable rate. An ad in your local paper or music store can also be useful. If you are good enough, age should not be a barrier.

3. *COPYIST*—If you are a musician with a good handwriting, you have a useful and profitable skill. Composers and arrangers often need their parts copied. Songwriters may also want a lead sheet written from their tape. A lead sheet contains the melody line, chord symbols, and words to a song. Advertise your services and keep your rates competitive.

4. *RECORD STORES*—A good training ground for young people who want to make a career in the music business. By learning about how records are distributed, sold, and returned, you are getting a firsthand look at this most important phase of the business.

5. *MUSIC STORES*—A good place to meet musicians and familiarize yourself with musical instruments and sheet music. If you are mechanical, you might also get involved in the minor repairs of instruments.

6. *INSTRUMENT AND EQUIPMENT REPAIR*—If you have the interest and talent, you might convince an experienced craftsman to let you become a part-time apprentice. You can also work for yourself, performing minor tasks like changing strings, raising guitar bridges, and soldering loose electrical connections for local bands.

7. *ROADIE*—If you do not play an instrument but want to get involved with a group, you can offer to handle the equipment for a local band. You might not ask for compensation if the band you are working with is just getting off the ground. But once they start getting paid, make sure that you get some kind of fee. Working with a band gives you a firsthand education in the music business.

8. *MANAGER/AGENT*—If you have a good head for business, offer your services to a local group. Tell them that you will handle their advertising and set prices with club owners and private parties who wish to hire the group. Many musicians would rather have someone else handle their business affairs. If you have a talent for this kind of work, it would be quite reasonable for you to receive a commission of 10–15 percent for all the work you line up.

9. *RECORDING STUDIOS*—If you have your eye on a career as a producer or recording engineer, try to get some kind of job in a local recording studio. Even if you start out sweeping floors, you will get a chance to learn how a studio operates. And if you have some real talent or potential, somebody is bound to notice.

10. *RADIO AND TELEVISION STATIONS*—Any kind of work that someone will let you do at a station is valuable experience. You must impress somebody that you are eager to learn the business and that you will be tickled pink to be a goffer, messenger, or anything else that the station requires. Remember the best way to enter a competitive career is to start at the bottom. And the time to start at the bottom is while you are still young.

Glossary

A&R (*Artist and Repertoire*).   The person with this title at a record company is usually involved with the finding and signing of acts.

Advance against royalties.   A sum paid to a writer, musician, composer, or producer against future sales or performance of their work(s).

Air check.   Tape of a disc jockey's show used for audition purposes or review by a radio station's program director.

Broadcast media.   Radio and television.

Contractor.   The person who hires musicians. Often a musician who may or may not play on the date he or she is booking.

Clout.   Power, prestige, influence, or pull.

Cover-copy.   A cover record is a re-recording of a previously released song. A cover band copies well-known hits.

Copyedit.   To correct and prepare a written work for typesetting and printing.

Copyright.   The right granted to a composer or writer for the exclusive publication, production, sale, and distribution of a musical work.

Demo. A demonstration recording used to present a performer or song.

Double. To play a second instrument in addition to the primary instrument a musician is hired to play.

Demographics. Population breakdown by age, sex, education, income, and other factors.

Exclusive agreement. A written contract that states that a particular service can be performed only through the manager, producer, or record company that is a party to the contract.

Freelance. A person who sells his or her services to an employer without a long-term commitment.

Format. The type of programming used by a radio station.

Goffer (or gopher). The person who is sent out to get things, as in go-for coffee.

Hype. An exaggerated description or advertising campaign of a person or product.

Lead sheet. The music, lyrics, and chords to a particular song.

Play list. The limited number of songs that a radio disc jockey must select from.

Performing rights. Composer rights for compositions played on radio, television, and live performances. These rights are governed by the three Performing Rights Organizations—BMI, ASCAP, and SESAC.

Print media. Newspapers and magazines.

Proofreading. To read against an original manuscript for corrections.

Score. A way of writing music that shows all the parts of an instrumental or vocal ensemble.

Sideman. A musician who is hired on for a particular date or tour.

Showcase. A live performance that serves as an audition. Some showcases are held in rehearsal halls.

Studio musician. A freelance musician who is hired to play in recording studios.

Vanity publishers. Publishers of songs or books who charge the writers for their services.

Bibliography

Anderson, Craig. *Home Recording for Musicians.* New York: Guitar Player Books, 1978.

Baskerville, David. *Music Business Handbook.* Denver: The Sherwood Company, 1979.

Bolles, Richard Nelson. *What Color Is Your Parachute?* Berkeley, California: Ten Speed Press, 1979.

"Careers And Music." *Music Educators Journal,* Vol. 63-Number 7, March 1977.

Carr, Janet Baker. *Evening at Symphony: A Portrait of the Boston Symphony Orchestra.* Boston: Houghton Mifflin, 1977.

Chapple, Steve, and Garofalo, Reebee. *Rock 'n' Roll Is Here To Pay: The History and Politics of the Music Business.* Chicago: Nelson-Hall, 1977.

Csida, Joseph. *The Music/Record Career Handbook.* New York: Billboard Publications, 1975.

Davis, Clive. *Clive: Inside the Record Business.* New York: William Morrow, 1975.

Degan, Clara, and Stearns, Betty, ed. *Careers in Music.* U.S.A.: American Music Conference, 1980.

Fornatel, Peter, and Mills, Joshua E. *Radio in the Television Age.* Woodstock, New York: The Overlook Press, 1980.

Frascogna, Jr., Xavier, M., and Hetherington, Lee H. *Successful Artist Management.* New York: Billboard Publications, 1978.

Gersohn, Fredric B., ed. *Counseling Clients in The Performing Arts.* New York: Practising Law Institute, 1975.

Hart, Phillip. *Orpheus in the New World.* New York: Norton, 1973.

Lambert, Dennis, with Zalkind, Ronald. *Producing Hit Records.* A Zadoc Book. New York: Schirmer Books, 1980.

Lieber, Leslie. *How To Form a Rock Group.* New York: Grosset and Dunlap, 1973.

Mitchell, Ronald. *Opera—Dead or Alive: Production, Performance and Enjoyment of Musical Theatre.* Madison, WI: University of Wisconsin Press, 1970.

Rachlin, Harvey. *The Songwriter's Handbook.* New York: Funk and Wagnalls, 1978.

Scheele, Adele. *Skills For Success.* New York: Ballantine Books, 1979.

Sehicke, C. A. *Revolution in Sound: A Biography of the Recording Industry.* Boston: Little, Brown, 1974.

Shemel, Sidney, and Krasilovsky, William M. *This Business of Music.* New York: Billboard Publications, 1978.

————. *More About This Business.* New York: Billboard Publications, 1978.

Stein, Howard, with Zalkind, Ronald. *Promoting Rock Concerts.* A Zadoc Book. New York: Schirmer Books, 1979.

Stokes, Geoffrey. *Starmaking Machinery.* New York: The Bobbs-Merrill Company, Inc., 1976.

Thomson, Virgil. *The Art of Judging Music.* New York: Alfred A. Knopf, 1958.

Weissman, Dick. *The Music Business: Career Opportunities and Self Defense.* New York: Crown Publishers, 1979.

Zalkind, Ronald, ed. *Contemporary Music Almanac 1980.* New York: Schirmer Books, 1980.

Index

About the Author

Gene Busnar is the author of the books *It's Rock 'n' Roll* and *Superstars of Rock,* and numerous magazine articles. He had been involved in the music business as a musician, songwriter, record producer, and teacher. Gene is currently working on a new book—*The Rhythm and Blues·Story*—and several related projects for radio and television.